Without God Nothing Makes Sense

Donald DeMarco

En Route Books and Media, LLC

Saint Louis, MO

Make the time

En Route Books and Media, LLC
5705 Rhodes Avenue
St. Louis, MO 63109

Contact us at contactus@enroutebooksandmedia.com

Cover Image: "Lord that I May See" by artist William Kurelek. Copyright: the Estate of William Kurelek, courtesy of the Wynick/Tuck Gallery, Toronto

Copyright 2024 Donald DeMarco

ISBN: 979-8-88870-294-9
Library of Congress Control Number: 2024952096

All rights reserved. No part of this book may be reproduced, stored in a retrieval system, or transmitted in any form, or by any means, electronic, mechanical, photocopying, or otherwise, without the prior written permission of the author.

This book is dedicated to
Our Lady of Guadalupe,
Patroness of the Unborn

My thanks to Tom, Peggy, Angie, Paul, Kristen, Anne, and Sebastian for their encouragement and support.

Quotations

"Life without God is like an unsharpened pencil—it has no point."

— Billy Graham

"If there is no God, everything is permitted."

— Dostoevsky

"Man can build a world without God but this world will end against him."

— Saint John Paul II

"Progress is Providence without God. That is, it is a theory that everything has always perpetually gone right by accident. It is based on an everlasting coincidence far more miraculous than a miracle."

— G. K. Chesterton

Table of Contents

Introduction 1

I. Language 5

    Chapter 1: The Unreliability of the Single Word 7

    Chapter 2: T-Shirt Philosophy 11

    Chapter 3: The Enthronement of the Lie.. 15

    Chapter 4: Do Not Judge 19

    Chapter 5: The Three Greatest Speeches 23

II. Morality... 27

    Chapter 6: Is Life Worth Living? 29

    Chapter 7: The Three Virtues of the Heart: Lightheartedness,
        Kindheartedness, and Warmheartedness.. 33

    Chapter 8: The Other Side of the Wall... 37

    Chapter 9: Religious Bigotry and the Constitution 41

    Chapter 10: Why America Has Shut the Door to Peace..................... 45

III. Education... 49

    Chapter 11: Dear Old Golden Rule Days.. 51

    Chapter 12: Manipulating Words For the Purpose of Manipulating
        Minds 55

    Chapter 13: Surprising Facts We Should Know about Fetal
        Development 59

    Chapter 14: Darwin's Dark Deprivation... 63

    Chapter 15: On the Subject of Miracles 67

IV. Philosophy 71

Chapter 16: Philosophy, Osmosis and Abortion 73

Chapter 17: The Paradox of the Human Being 81

Chapter 18: A Note on the Supreme Wisdom 85

Chapter 19: The Wisdom of Knowing When to Stop 89

Chapter 20: What is Existentialism? 93

V. Politics 97

Chapter 21: The Duality of Potentiality 99

Chapter 22: How Politics Can Smother Philosophy 103

Chapter 23: How to Destroy America 107

Chapter 24: The Fragility of Democracy 111

Chapter 25: The Radical Change in the Conscience of America 115

VI. Religion 119

Chapter 26: The Primacy of Faith 121

Chapter 27: Do We Need the Ten Commandments? 125

Chapter 28: Has Genesis Been Deconstructed? 129

Chapter 29: Who Is Left to Defend Genesis? 133

Chapter 30: A Brief Introduction to the Life of Edith Stein/ Saint Teresa Benedicta of the Cross 137

Epilogue: None Are So Blind 141

Introduction

Marlon Brando once remarked that when he takes his last breath, he will say to himself, "What was that all about!" Does death make a mockery out of life? Does it render life meaningless? Can anything make sense if death is the final act?

Brando, so to speak, had it all: devastating good looks, superb acting skills, wealth, fame, adulation, and a bundle of trophies. But all of this amounts to nothing if there is no God and no afterlife. We are situated between two infinities. We missed the previous one, we should not want to miss the next one.

Joan Crawford, another richly gifted celebrity, uttered her final words when her housekeeper had begun praying aloud at the actor's bedside: "Dammit, don't you dare ask God to help me." Disbelief in God as well as rejection of Him make life equally meaningless. The momentary pleasures expire the moment they are experienced.

The principal anxiety that characterizes the modern world is meaninglessness. For many, life has become an existential vacuum, devoid of a breath of meaning. Without God, Who is the source of all meaning, human beings engage in the hopeless attempt to create a heaven on earth. Such an endeavor is doomed to disappointment. As St. Augustine has pointed out, anything that is not eternal is too brief.

Our innate religious impulse inclines us to seek truth, wisdom, and God. When these impulses are denied, man becomes frustrated and yearns for something more fulfilling than pleasure, wealth, or fame. This book presents these frustrations in the areas of Language, Morality, Education, Philosophy, Politics, and Religion.

Language can be used for prayer, but it is often distorted to serve a secular ideology. Morality has been dissociated from nature and is replaced by Relativism. Education, instead of being guided by truth, conforms to political correctness. Contemporary philosophy, rather than read into reality, is content to deconstruct it. Politics, by assigning priority to economic concerns, creates the impression that man lives by bread alone. Religion, which is the foundation for universal brotherhood, is commonly regarded as a purely private matter.

Without God, man diminishes himself on each of these six levels. It is as if he chooses to go through life radically incomplete, cutting himself off from his better self. Ludwig Feuerbach, in his book, *The Essence of Christianity*, states that "The great turning point in history will be when man becomes aware that the only God for man is man himself: *Homo Homini, Deus!*" Henri De Lubac, S. J., on the other hand, in his carefully researched book, *The Drama of Atheist Humanism*, comes to the conclusion, agreeing with Dostoevsky, that "man cannot organize the world for himself without God; without God he can only organize the world *against man*. Exclusive humanism is inhuman humanism."

The cover, taken from William Kurelek's *Lord that I may see*, portrays the citizen of the world who needs light. The light, however, does not come from within, but from God. Let there be light so that I can see!

Without God, man becomes confused and his life makes little sense because a major piece of life's puzzle is missing. God is that missing piece and He is not difficult to locate. If we could only search our hearts, we should find Him.

December 12, 2024

Waterloo, Ontario

I.

Language

Chapter 1

The Unreliability of the Single Word

In his debate with J. D. Vance, Tim Walz told the world that the people of Minnesota are "pro-freedom". The truth is that no citizen of the Gopher state is pro-freedom. Life demands that we know when to stop. We must apply the brakes on freedom, or we run the risk of destroying everything. Freedom without restraint permits unfettered destruction.

Governor Walz's *faux pas,* squeezing a large idea into a nutshell is not unusual. 'Reproductive freedom' covers more ground than is possible. Infertility strikes many women who would like nothing more than to have a child. Where is their freedom to control their bodies? Reproductive technologies often go awry or simply fail. We are all finite beings. Our wishes are limited by our finitude. We have more control over our thoughts and actions than we have over our bodies. The control of our bodies is severely limited.

The single-word philosophy exemplifies verbal unreliability. It is unreliability, however, disguised as trustworthiness. It fits neatly on a T-shirt or on the lips of a public speaker. It also greets the ear with ease and remains firmly lodged in the memory. It purports to simplify life, but merely adds to its confusion.

Let us consider the word "equality." It is applied thoughtlessly to things that are clearly not equal. It presumes justice but delivers ambiguity. It is hardly a universal ideal. Alone, it is deceptive and often dangerous. Alexis de Tocqueville explains how equality can contain its very antithesis: "Democracy and socialism have nothing in common but one word, equality. But notice the difference: while democracy seeks equality in liberty, socialism seeks equality in restraint and servitude. When the past no longer illuminates the future, the spirit walks in darkness."

We can also divide "equality" into the mathematical and the limited kinds. Mathematically, 5=5 and 500=500. The sexes are equal in their humanity, but complementary in mission. It is a mistake to attempt to make them equal in every way since their equality is limited by their condition. The sexes are not absolutely equal. Nor is same-sex 'marriage' equal to a marriage between a man and a woman.

The word "change" has been employed by every politician who has ever run for office. The pursuit of perfection requires no end to changes. At the same time, change can move in a variety of directions, some good, others bad. We need change, but what kind of change is it that we do need? The Third Reich represented a change, but that change required a greater change. And on and on history goes, one change after another, sometimes beneficial, other times disastrous. The word 'change' does not include a blessing.

Currently, "racism" is used recklessly. Mathematics, for example, is said to be racist, as well as biology, literature scripture, and even the English language. The distinguished economist Thomas Sowell states, with both insight and humor, that, "The word 'racism' is like ketchup. It can be put on practically anything—and demanding evidence makes you a 'racist'." What does it mean to be called a 'racist'? Does it sting or does it provoke a shrug? It is simply another example of how the single-word is unable to convey a coherent meaning.

Chapter 1: The Unreliability of the Single Word

"Progress" is met with near reverence. It is "Our most important product," according to the motto of General Electric. It baptizes our collective illusion that everything is getting better all the time. Yet, as G. K. Chesterton has pointed out, "The concept of progress acts as a protective mechanism to shield us from the terrors of the future." The incomparable essayist also declared the "Progress is a comparative about which we have not settled the superlative." Progress does not tell us where we are going, but only that things are changing. As a single word philosophy, it leaves us in the dark. It betrays the proper function of the word as enlightening.

'Compassion' is another example of a word that is both constantly misunderstood and therefore constantly misused. Abortion advocates use it to buttress their argument for abortion. It is stretched beyond its literal meaning to advance a moral preference. Compassion refers to the ability to feel another's pain. It is, by no means, a reason to abort. "The dew of compassion is a tear," wrote Lord Byron, "but the 'do' of compassion is 'unclear'." Compassion is a feeling, not a prescription of a particular action.

When a person claims to have a 'right', he seems to be in possession of something incontestable. It stops any argument in its tracks. Yet, a right may be grounded in the natural law, having relevance for everyone. Or it may be plucked out of thin air and used for political purposes. The 'right' to life and the alleged 'right' to abortion cannot mean the same thing. A 'right' cannot be a wrong, no more than a wrong can be a 'right'. The heedless use of the word 'right' can lead to mayhem.

The ancient Greeks had some wise words concerning the use of words, "Words empty as the wind," said Homer, "are best left unsaid." It is a wise man who knows when to be silent. And Socrates advised that "False words are not only evil in themselves, but they infect the soul with evil." Language is not merely a literary phenomenon, it has a moral quality. The day will come when we will be judged by our words. We must be careful not to misuse our words, but to communicate their richness.

Chapter 2

T-Shirt Philosophy

A friend of mine who teaches theology at a Catholic University informed me of an unforgettable experience he had on a flight to Chicago to visit an old friend. Seated next to him was a young woman wearing a t-shirt identifying herself as a proud member of the "pro-choice generation." My friend wanted to say to her, "Lucky for you your mother wasn't a member." He said nothing, a "moment of cowardice I now regret." But he continues to send prayers her way.

Does this young woman have any respect for the meaning of the word "generation." She is, whether she realizes it or not, the consequence of a long line of generations that lead back to our first parents. All her preceding generations said "yes" to life. Now, she says "no"! But why? What can be greater than life? According to her t-shirt philosophy, it is "choice".

"Choice" is a body without legs. It does not go anywhere! One might as well have a t-shirt that says, "Go". But, one may ask, "Go where?" Go crazy, go to church, go away, go rogue? "Choice" is dangling in the air destitute of any connection to anything. We do not see t-shirts sporting the word "Go" no more than we see them with the word "Stop". No one is either "pro-go" or "pro-stop". These words are much too indefinite to have any meaning, let alone inspire a nationwide movement.

My friend explained how implausible it is to boast of being a member of a "generation" whose philosophy is, in itself, indecipherable. As he informed me: "It is astonishing to me that even after fifty years of hearing the same tired old shibboleth, the pro-choice crowd continues to trot it out as if it were a thunderbolt fallen from the sky. To them, the argument is as fresh and delicious as this morning's first cup from Starbucks." Well phrased and philosophically impeccable!

No one is against choice if that word merely expresses the capacity to make choices. Thus, "choice" is not an issue. There is absolutely no need for a pro-choice movement. What is at issue is *what is chosen*. Advertisers are in love with the word "affordable." Every senior residence, for example, is "affordable". But it is affordable only to those who can afford it. "Affordable" dangles in the air and to whom it applies is unspecified. It surely does not apply to everyone.

If I were in this ticklish situation that my friend experienced on the airplane, what might I have said to the young lady? "Excuse me, but I am fascinated by the statement on your t-shirt. But I have a question. "Do you include me in your membership? I have chosen to ask you this question and I am wondering if, in asking it, I am out of bounds?" She would extend to me the right to choose this question. Then, I would ask her another question. "Do you realize that your pro-choice philosophy is identical with that of Adolph Hitler's because he was also pro-choice in feeling free to choose exterminating the Jews?" She would then become indignant and insist that there are limits to choice. I would then suggest that she modify her t-shirt slogan by adding the words, "with restrictions." "You, nor

Chapter 2: T-Shirt Philosophy

anybody else is simply "pro-choice." "Your t-shirt is a lie!" I have now angered my co-passenger, and she begs me to leave her alone.

"Please let me ask you just one more question," I would entreat, "since I am trying to understand your position." Is something good because it is chosen or is something chosen because it is good"? My question would puzzle her and I would need to rephrase it. "Does your mother love you because you are loveable or are you loveable because she has chosen to love you?" She changes the subject because she is not sure that her mother really loves her. I continue to explain by pointing out that it is not being chosen that makes one good. If that were the case, then we would be bereft of any shred of goodness that is our own, certainly a condition that could not make us proud. We are loved because we are originally something that is good. Love is a response to that goodness not its creator. So too, our ability to choose should be directed to something that is good. The abortion issue is not about choice, but about whether the unborn child is something good that we should not seek to destroy. If you were upfront about your position, your t-shirt should read, "I am in favor of the choice to kill unborn children." That would be honest. But it would never sell. You are a member of an advertising firm that wants people to think that your movement is better than it really is.

There is an element of cowardice in being pro-choice by concealing what is chosen. There is also an element of respect for life in the fact that the odious word "abortion" is an affront to respect for life.

These words may not have been convincing. The promotion of abortion requires the abandonment of reason. Being pro-life and being pro-reason coincide. Nonetheless, it is everyone's moral obligation to stand up for reason and condemn its abuse.

I find myself to be an invisible co-passenger with my friend in his flight to Chicago and will join him in prayer for the misguided young woman he encountered

Chapter 3

The Enthronement of the Lie

There is an old Russian saying that a lie can get around the world faster than one can get his boots on. The lie, being a half-truth, can travel faster than the truth which is weighed down by its complexity. In addition, the pleasant lie is more appealing than the naked truth. Hence its popularity. "The truth will make you odd," warned Flannery O'Connor. Nonetheless, she lived by it because she found strength in Christ's declaration that He is the "Truth".

The clash between the popular lie and the burdensome truth is nowhere better found than in the career of Jordan B. Peterson. He is "the most important and influential Canadian thinker since Marshall McLuhan," writes Camille Paglia. And yet he is the most "despicable" man in the world, say his detractors and pegged a "right-wing extremist".

Norman Doidge, who is a psychiatrist, psychoanalyst, and author of *The Brain that Changes Itself* and *The Brain's Way of Healing*, has said, "With all the moderation that I can summon," that if one is looking for "the kind of person with the comprehension, tools, good will and courage to combat [right-wing bigotry], "Jordan Peterson is *that* man.

Early in his career as a clinical psychologist, Peterson came to the realization "that almost everything I said was untrue". He wanted to win arguments, gain status, and twist the world into what he thought it should be. He was, in his own words, a "fake". But what was he to do. His personal decision was to "tell the truth". And so that was the path he would take throughout his career. "Truth," he would go on to state in is best-selling book, *12 Rules for Life: An Antidote to Chaos,* "is the ultimate, inexhaustible natural resource. It's the light in the darkness".

One is not obliged to tell the truth in all circumstances, but enthroning the lie is unconscionable. But there are times when the truth must be told. In an exclusive statement he made for LifeSite News, Peterson stated that radical LGBT activists are working to destroy Catholicism. He condemned the "Catholic" school system in Canada for embracing the LGBT agenda and blasted Catholics who succumb to the demands of the LGBT "mob". "The radical LGBTETC agenda," he said, "couldn't be more antithetical to Catholic doctrine if it had been specifically designed for that purpose". "The radicals within the alphabet movement," he added, "are trying to do to Catholicism more narrowly and Christianity more broadly what they do to all traditions: destroy them. They use guilt, manipulation . . . along with constant claims of victimization and oppression. "Catholics too asleep or naive to notice or gulled into cooperating because of appeals to compassion are the 'useful idiots' participating in their own demise".

It us sheer naivete on the part of certain Catholic School Board members and even presidents of Catholic colleges to misinterpret the LGBTQ+ message that God embraces everyone. That God embraces everyone is a basic tenet of the Church. It does not need to be reiterated in a fragmentary way focusing exclusively on sexual deviancy. Where are the carpenters, electricians, lawyers, bakers, and postal workers? The rainbow flag is not inclusive; it is exclusive. Pederson is right, though most certainly politically incorrect.

Chapter 3: The Enthronement of the Lie

Peterson is not Catholic, though he sounds more Catholic than many Catholics. Nonetheless, he recognizes and values the Catholicism and its rich tradition. He calls on Catholics to fight to preserve their faith. In so stating he is more episcopal than many Catholic bishops.

Alexander Solzhenitsyn was also an outspoken champion of the truth. "One word of truth outweighs the world," he famously stated. In his own country, Russia, the lie was not simply a moral category "but a pillar of the state". There will be lies, he realized, but he felt the responsibility to prevent the lie from coming through him. In this respect, Solzhenitsyn and Peterson have much in common, doing what one can for a higher purpose. "It is the artist who realizes that there is a supreme force above him and works gladly away as a small apprenticeship under God's heaven."

In his book, *The New Tower of Babel*, Dietrich von Hildebrand has a chapter entitled, "*The Dethronement of Truth*. "One of the most ominous features of the present epoch", "he writes, "is undoubtedly the dethronement of truth". The consequence of this dethronement is not a moral vacuum or a lawless society, but the enthronement of the lie. This ascendancy of the lie is pernicious in the extreme. It aims at depriving people of their right to know the truth and to establish a realistic basis, common to all, in their attempt to establish a just society. Although von Hildebrand focuses in the more drastic dethronements of truth in Nazism and in atheistic communism, he recognizes that this same disregard can occur in democratic countries. Truth, he states, cannot be a mere personal opinion. It is a conformity with reality. Democracy cannot succeed if all opinions are considered equal while the truth remains unacknowledged and unemployed.

Truth is not unattainable nor is foreign to our deepest instincts. "O Truth, Truth," cried St. Augustine, "how inwardly did the very marrow of my soul pant for You" (*The Confessions of St. Augustine,* (III, 6). Truth belongs to human beings as much as it belongs to God. The lie is contrary to the dignity of man and is an offense against God. The enthronement of truth should be society's noblest and most important goal.

Chapter 4

Do Not Judge

Christ is firm concerning judging others. In Matthew 7, 1-5, He commands us, "Do not judge, that you may not be judged. For with what judgment you judge, you shall be judged, and with what measure you measure it shall be measured to you. But why dost thou see the speck in thy brother's eye, and yet dost not consider the beam in thy own eye?"

This council is critically needed since it is all too common for people to judge one another. Judging another presupposes a position of moral superiority. This explains why we make ourselves vulnerable when we judge others. Pride, of course, anticipates a fall. Our standard of judging others will be the same standard by which we will be judged. This fearful proposition should give us pause. There are dire consequences to overlooking our own faults and presuming that we have the ability to judge the motives of others.

If the word "beam" (sometimes translated as "log" or "plank") seems to be an exaggeration, it is justified in terms of the comparative magnitude of the judger's faults and those whom he criticizes. Nathaniel Hawthorne's novel, *The Scarlet Letter*, is set in 17th century Massachusetts where Hester Prynne is forced to wear the letter "A" to indicate that she had, presumably, committed adultery. She is harshly judged by the Puritan mindset of the townsfolk. Those who presumed to judge her seemed oblivious to their own hypocrisy.

Hawthorne understood that the hypocrisy of the Puritans who condemned Hester Prynne set in motion their own punishment. "No man, wrote Hawthorne, "for any considerable period, can wear one face to himself, and another to the multitude, without finally getting bewildered as to which may be the true…" Being two-faced leads can lead to the loss of one's personal identity.

Joan of Arc, who was the victim of an outrageously wrong-headed judgment, warned her accusers of the price that would be on their heads: "You say that you are my judge; I do not know if you are; but take good heed not to judge me ill, because you would put yourself in great peril."

The *Scarlet Letter* brings to mind the passage in John 8, 7 concerning the woman caught in adultery who was brought to Jesus by the Scribes and Pharisees. Jesus was asked whether He agreed, according to the command of Moses, that she should be stoned to death. But Jesus, stooping down, began to write with His finger on the ground. The Scribes and Pharisees, however, continued to pressure Jesus. Finally, He said to them, "Let him who is without sin among you be the first to cast a stone at her". After her detractors left, Jesus said to the woman that He would not condemn her, but from now on she should "sin no more".

It is important that we not over-extend the meaning of "Judge not" to include the legitimate use of the mind in judging ideas, whether they are correct or erroneous, actions, whether they are good or bad, and propositions, whether they are true or false. We need to make judgments in these matters in order to help people. For Aquinas, "The greatest kindness one can render to any man consists in leading him to truth".

Chapter 4: Do Not Judge

Sheer ignorance would be of no help to anyone. But we are neighbors to each other and inherit the solemn obligation to be of help to each other, especially on the road to salvation. We are, in fact, required to use our minds to assist others as we navigate through the various obstacle that life has set before us.

The day will come when God will judge each one of us. But who we are in the eyes of God is not someone that any one of us can know. It is in this sense that the command, "Do not judge" has its decisive meaning. Jacques Maritain, in his book, *On the Use of Philosophy*, expresses the matter accurately and beautifully: "But we are utterly forbidden to judge the innermost heart, that inaccessible center where the person day after day weaves his own fate and ties the bonds binding him to God. When it comes to that, there is only one thing to do, and that is to trust God. And that is precisely what love for our neighbor prompts is to do".

It is tempting to misinterpret the command, "Do not judge" and refrain from all legitimate judgments. Thus, many take refuge in the fraudulent excuse, "Who am I to judge?" This is not a case of being kind to people by not judging their actions. It is actually a case of failing to exercise our duty to be of assistance to them. The natural law offers us a reliable basis for making moral judgments. The ultimate purpose of education is to develop our inherent capacities to distinguish between truth and error. Being open-minded does not mean to remain open even when convincing evidence has been presented. The truly open-minded person remains open to the truth until he apprehends it.

The rule of law could not be enforced without a judge. It is the responsibility of the judge to render a verdict concerning one's innocence of guilt. And it is good to remember that the word verdict derives from two Latin words, *verum* and *dicere* meaning to tell the truth. In addition, witnesses are obliged to swear that their testimony is truthful. Without an agreement as to what constitutes the truth, society would collapse.

Chapter 5

The Three Greatest Speeches

It is a daunting task to come up with the three greatest speeches of all time. Nevertheless, people love lists, as attested to by the immense success of any of the three *Book of Lists* compiled by David Wallechinsky, his father, Irving Wallace, and sister Amy Wallace. Our passion for lists is one important way in which we human beings differ from primates.

My choice for the three greatest speeches, in order, is Lincoln's "Gettysburg Address," Winston Churchill's "Blood, Sweat and Tears," and Martin Luther King, Jr.'s "I Have a Dream". I did not include the Sermon on the Mount despite its monumental significance because I regard it as a "sermon" rather than as a "speech". This list will not meet with universal agreement, but it may be a good starting point for animated discussion. Nonetheless, we may ask, what three speeches were more influential than the triad that I propose. I rest my case.

On second thought, however, and as the result of doing some investigative research, I must defer to that supreme list maker, Ignatius, the third Bishop of Antioch, who was born in Syria around the year 35 AD and is believed to have been a student of St. John the Apostle. If there is any quarreling about the three greatest speeches, Ignatius has put the issue to rest for all time. The good bishop of Antioch has proposed that the three greatest speeches of all time belong to the same orator, namely, God.

Now, if God is the "Word," we should expect that He would speak. Furthermore, His speaking would be arranged as speeches. And what are His three greatest speeches? The first Speech was delivered on Day One and is rather lengthy both in time and in space. In fact, it is perpetually available to us. In a word, for Bishop Ignatius, it is Creation.

In order to listen to this speech, we must be silent. Creation is an unusual form of speech because we do not hear it directly, but through the animals, plants, stars, planets, in their various modes of limited expression. Therefore, we hear the speech of Creation indirectly through God's creatures and everything else he created.

The besetting sin of the modern world is the reduction of Creation to mere nature. This effectively shuts out God's voice. Best-selling author, Richard Dawkins, author of *The God Delusion*, contends that at bottom, the universe is "nothing but blind, pitiless indifference". Philosopher Daniel Dennett, author of *Breaking the Spell: Religion as a Natural Phenomenon*, concludes that DNA, a "mindless scrap of molecular machinery, is the ultimate basis of all agency, and hence meaning, and hence consciousness, in the universe".

The second of the three greatest speeches for Ignatius is "Scripture" in which God speaks directly to man. However, certain scholars have reduced the Word of God to a mere collection of historical texts that are no longer relevant in today's world. Scripture, then, is liberally re-interpreted, revised, and de-constructed. The Bible, for many, is out of date and its adherents may face fines or even imprisonment for quoting specific passages that do not square with contemporary preferences.

The Bible, consequently, is reduced to literature and is regarded as having no more authority than anyone's opinion. And so, the modern world is blind to the fact that the Bible is a Speech that is offered to us by God.

Finally, the third of the greatest speeches is the Incarnation. Here, the Word is given flesh in the form of Christ as a human being. It is the culmination of God's speaking to us and responds to our deepest hunger. Unfortunately, those who understand this third Speech are criticized as backward, illiberal, and irrelevant. The "liberal" view of the Incarnation welcomes a remodeled Christ who emphasizes the importance of this world, while downplaying the next.

God's first Speech speaks to man's senses, the second to his intellect, the third to his heart. The rejection of each of these Speeches is tantamount to a rejection of one's self. Without the proper operation of his senses, intellect, and heart, man ceases to be man. The three Speeches affirm man in his wholeness. By being blind or deaf to each of these speeches results in a rejection of both man and God. Here is the great tragedy of the modern world. "We are no longer able to hear God," commented Pope Benedict XVI. "There are too many different frequencies filling our ears". The only frequency to which we should tune our ears is the one that is broadcast from Heaven.

Each of God's three Speeches are important forms of communication. In ascending order, the first elicits reverence, the recognition that the created world is majestic and inspires awe. The second, in accord with the Ten Commandments, commands obedience to God's law. The third Speech directs us to love God and neighbor.

Together they provide all that is needed for human beings to fulfill themselves and, at the same time, be united with their Creator.

Creative listening is our surest road to personal happiness. And yet, we persist in listening to the voice of the world urging us to be independent and do things "our way". In the silence that comes from humility, we begin to see the God-given beauty of nature, the wisdom of scripture, and the Love of Jesus Christ. We may begin listening to God by first listening to the wisdom of Bishop Ignatius of Antioch.

II.

Morality

Chapter 6

Is Life Worth Living?

In February 1952, Bishop Sheen began a series of television talks that proved to be, over time, immensely successful. In that year he won an Emmy for Most Outstanding Television Personality, beating out Lucille Ball, Arthur Godfrey, Edward R. Murrow, and Jimmy Durante. His show competed effectively against shows starring Milton Berle and Frank Sinatra.

Sheen changed the original title of his show from *Is Life Worth Living?* to the more positive sounding, *Life Is Worth Living*. He also wrote a series of books under that title. In 1952, 75% of Americans told pollsters that religion was "very important" in their lives. This percentage has dwindled significantly since then justifying a reversal of the question back to the original *Is Life Worth Living*? The definitive answer has been replaced by the searching question. A 2024 poll indicates that 45% of Americans find religion to be an important part of their lives.

Today, abortion and suicide take a heavy toll of human lives. In Canada, euthanasia has been increasing dramatically. Since Canada legalized Medical Assistance in Death (MAiD) in 2016, there have been 44,958 reported cases of MAiD with a growth rate of 31.2% since 2021. There is no indication that the rate is slowing down.

There may be a close connection between the decline of religion and a decline of enthusiasm for life. Christ said, "I came that they may have life and have it abundantly" (John 10:10). God is both the Creator of life and its promoter. To be on the side of God is to be on the side of life. Turning away from God means turning to oneself. But we must die to oneself in order to live more abundantly. In John 12:24-26, we read: "Truly, truly, I say to you, unless a grain of wheat falls into the earth and dies, it remains alone; but if it dies, it bears much fruit. Whoever loves his life loses it, and whoever hates his life in this world will keep it for eternal life. If anyone serves me, he must follow me; and where I am, there will my servant be also. If anyone serves me, the Father will honor him."

Henry Wadsworth Longfellow's greatest poem, *A Psalm to Life,* is akin to a motivational speech to rouse people out of their lethargy. In the seventh quatrain he states: "Lives of great men all remind us/We can make our lives sublime,/And, departing leave behind us/Footprints on the sands of time."

Catholics may associate "great men" with the saints who lived life abundantly, though many of them had to deal with great suffering and acute disappointment. It is also important to remember that a person's life affects posterity. A life well lived leaves "footprints on the sands of time" thereby benefiting people in the future. A good life can benefit others in all directions. Thinking too much of oneself is to smother the generosity of the soul. We do not exist for ourselves alone. By thinking of others, we expand our existence and discover reasons to keep on living. Life is worth living and therefore the effort is worth making to ensure that its worth is realized. Without effort, life has no rapture.

Steven Pinker, a noted Harvard psychologist, penned an article entitled *The Stupidity of Dignity* (*The New Republic,* May 2008). He proposes that "dignity" should be scrapped and replaced by 'autonomy.' Ironically, secularists employ the word 'dignity' in promoting

Chapter 6: Is Life Worth Living?

euthanasia. It would be a grave mistake, however, to deny the dignity of the human being. Dignity is conferred by God who has created man in his own image. It indicates the special value of the human being that raises him far above the notion of being a mere individual. Because man has dignity, he cannot be used as an object, nor can he be assaulted. It means that he is inviolate. On the other hand, reducing him to an autonomous being both denies him his dignity while depriving him of his wholeness. The 'self-made man,' the man who relies on himself alone is an illusion. Man by nature is a social being. He is created to love and involve himself in positive relationships with others. Life cannot be worth living when a person cuts himself off from others and attempts to live an independent or autonomous existence.

Being autonomous appeals to pride. We are often attempted to think that we are better than we are. But pride is the condition that precipitates a fall. Illusions are not sustainable. And a fall is not pleasant. By contrast, humility is based on a realistic understanding of who we are. Life is worth living for those who know who they are—not self-sufficient, but not without worth—and have faith in God.

The temptation to think that life is not worth living gives death its appeal. Yet, we must ask, "What is there apart from life?" Only death and nothingness. In his encyclical *The Gospel of Life*, John Paul II stated that "Life is indelibly marked by a *truth of its own*." This means that life is a gift that conveys a mandate. "By accepting God's gift," he goes on to say, "man is obliged to *maintain life in this truth* which is essential to it. To detach oneself from this truth is to condemn oneself to meaninglessness and unhappiness . . ."

We are solemnly obliged to value life. But this obligation is not a burden for we soon realize that it is indeed worth living for it is a fount of meaningfulness and personal joy.

Chapter 7

The Three Virtues of the Heart: Lightheartedness, Kindheartedness, and Warmheartedness

The virtues of lightheartedness, kindheartedness, and warmheartedness can easily be related to the three persons of the Blessed Trinity. We may think of God the Father in terms of light. The Father as Creator is the first person of the Trinity to manifest His presence in the world. "Let there be light" calls the universe into being. Light has several meaning ranging from levity to illumination. The heart of the Father must be filled with light in order for light to emanate from Him. In this sense we may regard Him as lighthearted.

If we understand kindheartedness as caring for others in a gentle manner, it is easy to apply this virtue to Christ whose relationships with others, especially with women, was unfailingly kind. Ephesians 4:32 tells us to "Be kind and compassionate to one another, forgiving each other, just as in Christ God forgave you." Christ was the epitome of kindheartedness.

The Holy Spirit appeared to the apostles as "tongues of fire" when they were confirmed in grace so that they could carry out Christ's mission. John the Baptist predicted that Jesus will be the one who "baptizes you with the Holy Spirit and with fire" (Matthew 3:11). Fire purifies and also denotes passion, factors that that lift Christians out of their lethargy. The fire of the Holy Spirit, unlike ordinary fires, is inextinguishable.

Lightheartedness:

G. K. Chesterton famously stated that angels can fly because they take themselves lightly. Nothing is more depressing than being weighed down by an oppressive ego. Charles Dickens' immortal tale, *A Christmas Carol,* is about the conversion of Ebenezer Scrooge's heart from being heavy to light. "I am a light as a feather," he remarks. "I am as happy as an angel, I am as merry as a school boy." Christmas is a time of light, merriment, and joy. The glow of the Christmas tree invites everyone to be lighthearted.

Lightness in the form of levity picks us up. It helps us to fly. We are positioned between two diametrically opposed forces: grace and gravity. Gravity weighs us down; levity acts as grace and picks us up. Dostoevsky once said that the laughter of children is a "ray of sunshine from paradise." There must be laughter in heaven. "A light heart lives long," wrote Shakespeare. If laughter is out best medicine, lightheartedness is its serving tray.

Kindheartedness:

Random acts of kindness has become a popular trend. There is simply too much misery and gloom in the world. And, sadly, too many random acts of violence. It is a wonderful thing to be surprised by kindness. Kindheartedness flows from a generous heart. Because it is not required, it is all the more admirable. A kind word can brighten the day. It costs nothing and offends no one. And it is contagious. One act of kindness inspired another. What Shakespeare said about mercy can also be applied to kindness—it is "not strained." This characteristic speaks to its naturalness. It is as natural as mother's milk and virtually as nourishing. American author, Washington Irving, expressed the matter most eloquently when he noted, "How truly is a kind heart a fountain of gladness, making everything in its vicinity to freshen into smiles."

Scripture repeatedly reminds us of the fundamental importance of being kind. St. Peter advises us to "put away all malice and all guile and insincerity and envy and all slander. Like new born babes, long for the spiritual milk, that by it you may grow up to salvation; for you have tasted the kindness of the Lord" (1 Peter 2:1-3). Scripture itself is kind to us.

Warmheartedness:

The human heart is like a fireplace that sends its warmth to comfort those who huddle around it. It is the perfect antidote for our "winter of discontent". Warmheartedness is a virtue that is better associated with older people. According to New England novelist, John P. Marquand, "There is a certain phase in the life of the aged when the warmth of the heart seems to increase in direct proportion with years."

The person of warmheartedness is never ruffled by trivia. He is comfortable and focusses on the important features of life. He embraces the family and dotes on his grandchildren. Ambition gives way to relaxation. Disagreements no longer trouble him. His advice is always seasoned with love. His warmheartedness is the afterglow of a life well spent.

Phyllis McGinley, in her poem, *Midcentury Love Letter*, refers to how urgent it is for the love between husband and wife to continue as they move into their advanced years, to "breathe each other warm." The warmth of the heart keeps the fire of love from extinguishing. Recall how the two travelers on the road to Emmaus were affected when they walked with and listened to the words of Christ: "Were not our hearts burning within us while he talked with us on the road and opened the Scriptures to us" (Luke 24:13-35)?

The Holy Trinity is the consolidation of lightheartedness, kindheartedness, and warmheartedness. As we practice this trinity of virtues, we become more godlike. At the same time, we can chart a person's life through the levity of youth, the kindness of the adult, and the warmth of the elderly. It may be a rare individual who possesses all three of these virtues at the same time. Yet they abide together in God forever.

Chapter 8

The Other Side of the Wall

An associate of mine, a medical doctor who specializes in organ transplants, took his son to the United States Holocaust Memorial Museum in Washington. He fully expected that the visit would teach his young son an important lesson concerning both history and humanity. The lesson he learned, however, was altogether different than the one that was expected.

The lad was wearing a pro-life T-shirt. This was enough to disqualify him from entering the museum. His father's protests were in vain. Being pro-life does not contradict the museum's essential message. It parallels it. It is yet another example of man's inhumanity to man on a large scale. Roughly a million abortions a year were being performed in the United States at that time. The slogan "never again" should apply equally to the abortion Holocaust.

John Powell, S. J. saw fit to title his critique of abortion, *Abortion, the Silent Holocaust*. He argues that since the abortion holocaust is only too real, to deny it is tantamount to being a holocaust denier. The denial, unfortunately, is widespread and repudiates the message that the Museum is trying to communicate. There is no museum dedicated to the millions of unborn babies who were and continue to be victims of mass extermination.

Zone of Interest is a film that won an Academy Award in 2023 for the Best International Feature Film. It centers on Rudolf Höss, commandant of Auschwitz, and his family. The atrocities going on in the concentration camp do not seem to disturb the Höss family although their domicile is separated from the camp by a mere wall. Mrs. Höss maintains what appears to be a happy home. She has a garden which produces herbs for cooking. The children have a pool where they frolic and play. The father reads bedtime stories to the youngest of their brood.

The distance that separates the Höss family and the horrors that are taking place in the concentration camp is less than twenty yards. From a psychic perspective, the distance is infinite. How is it possible, the viewer may ask himself, that on one side of the wall a Holocaust it raging while on the other side of the wall, a family is enjoying life? Mrs. Höss is not ignorant of what is transpiring on the other side of the wall. She uses human ashes from the Auschwitz ovens to fertilize the flowerbeds which are a source of pride for her. Hedwig's capacity for denial and her ability to close her mind and heart to the neighboring barbarities is shocking. And yet, shocking as it is, it is by no means unique. Human beings have the capacity for great evil as well as ignoring it and going on living as if it did not exist.

In his Academy Awards acceptance speech, director Jonathan Glazer referred to the timeliness of his film. He found it to be timely since, he maintained, it is applicable to what is transpiring in Israel and Gaza. He did not speak about its timeliness with regard to its application to the abortion holocaust.

Jason Morgan is an associate professor at Reitaku University in Kashiwa, Japan. He contends, in referring to the magnitude of abortion, that, "No film critic, to my knowledge, has acknowledged in a review the ongoing holocaust that has turned the United States into a living nightmare since 1973". People drive by or walk by abortion

Chapter 8: The Other Side of the Wall

clinics indifferent to the slaughter that goes on which seems oblivious to the world.

The abortion holocaust is, in a sense, more frightening than what took place at Auschwitz and other concentration camps because it is *our* holocaust. It touches home too deeply. We cannot bear the thought that we could engineer a holocaust of our own. And so, we deny what it is and separate our minds from it. It is not a holocaust, we insist, it is nothing more than women's reproductive freedom writ large. Indeed, it is something to celebrate.

The serene indifference of man to the plight of his fellow man is a moral pathology. History has taught us that *Homo homini lupus est* (man is a wolf to his fellow man). But we also know, to cite the Roman playwright, Terence, *Homo sum; humani nihil a me alienum puto* (I am human; I consider nothing human alien to me).

We preserve our humanness by our concern for everyone. To lapse into indifference toward others is to truncate our humanity. Pro-life advocates will continue to suffer many defeats as the battle goes on. But they are resilient and will rise to fight again, and again. The one defeat they cannot endure is to lose their regard for others, even those whom they do not know, and relapse into a comfortable life. Pro-lifers, by keeping alive that very concern for others, will ensure that they will not sink into a cold-heartedness that compromises their humanity.

Mahatma Gandhi's words invite serious reflection, "All humanity is one undivided and indivisible family, and each one of us is responsible for the misdeeds of all the others." We are not responsible for causing the misdeeds of others, but we are obliged not to ignore them. We were, each one of us, created by the same God. Therefore, we owe it to Him to love all His children. Being pro-life embraces everyone. To excuse evil is to make a deal with the devil.

Chapter 9

Religious Bigotry and the Constitution

The United States Constitution is quite friendly toward Catholics as well as towards all people who hold religious beliefs. Article VI, clause 3, states that "no religious Test shall ever be required as a Qualification to any Office or public Trust under the United States."

In a 1787 article defending the necessity of the Constitution's ban on religious tests, Oliver Ellsworth, third Chief Justice of the Supreme Court, defined a religious test as an act to be done, among other things, "for the purpose of determining whether his religious opinions are such that he is admissible to a public office." This clause is cited by advocates of separation of church and state as an example of the "original intent" of the framers of the constitution to avoid any confusion concerning the boundaries of the church and the state or involving the government in any way as a determiner of religious beliefs or practices. The secular world cannot ordain Catholic priests, nor can the church appoint secular officials. This clause is also significant because it represents the words of the original Framers, even prior to the Establishment Clause of the First Amendment.

By dramatic contrast, a variety of Test Acts were instituted in England during the 17th and 18th centuries. The chief purpose of the Tests was to exclude anyone who was not a member of the Church of England.

A variety of Test Acts were instituted in England during that period. Their main purpose was to exclude anyone not a member of the Church of England from holding government office (notably

Catholics and "non-conforming Protestants). Government officials were required to swear oaths, such as the Oath of Supremacy attesting that the monarch of England was the head of the Church and that they possessed no other foreign loyalties, such as to the pope. Such laws were common throughout Europe, wherever countries had a state religion.

The United States Constitution forbids such a Test. Therefore, a person cannot be disqualified from assuming an official post because he is Catholic or a member of any other religion. Nonetheless Act VI, clause 3 is not always honored in practice. During the 2020 senate hearing concerning Amy Coney Barrett's confirmation to the Supreme Court, her Catholicism was questioned. California Senator Dianne Feinstein stated that the candidate's Catholicism was a problem. "The dogma lives loudly within you," she said, "and that's of concern." Coney Barrett was confirmed by a vote of 52-48. All the Republicans except one voted in her favor, while all the Democrats and the two Independents voted against her.

Had Feinstein violated the Constitution's Article VI, clause three? Some critics believed her questioning was both unconstitutional as well as anti-Catholic. Feinstein defended herself by insisting that Barrett's writings were informed by her faith and thus were an obstacle to her service to her country. The great merit of the Constitution's ban on using a religious Test to determine a candidate's suitability for office is that it is a barrier against prejudice. A person's faith in God, for example, does not mean that he is incapable of serving the cause of justice. At the same time, a person's color does not indicate his proficiency or insufficiency in other areas. "Let us judge people not by the color of their skin, but by the content of their character," said Martin Luther King.

As Vice-President, Mike Pence once put senator Kamala Harris on the spot for her attacks on the religious views of several recent judicial nominees. "Senator," he said, "I know one of our judicial nominees you actually attacked, because they [sic] were a member of the Catholic Knights of Columbus just because the Knights of Columbus hold pro-life views. My hope is that when the hearing [Supreme Court Justice nomination] takes place that Judge Amy Coney Barrett will be respectfully voted and confirmed onto the Supreme Court of the United States." Harris voted against Barrett's confirmation. Questioning the suitability for office because of one's religious beliefs, however, is not uncommon in the world of politics.

In late 2018 Kamala Harris grilled Brian Buescher, who was nominated to be a federal district judge in Nebraska, about his membership in the Knights of Columbus, a Catholic fraternal organization with more than 2 million members worldwide that conducts charitable work. The following is one of Harris's written questions to Buescher:

"Since 1993, you have been a member of the Knights of Columbus, an all-male society comprised primarily of Catholic men. In 2016, Carl Anderson, leader of the Knights of Columbus, described abortion as 'a legal regime that has resulted in more than 40 million deaths.' Mr. Anderson went on to say that 'abortion is the killing of the innocent on a massive scale.' Were you aware that the Knights of Columbus opposed a woman's right to choose when you joined the organization?"

Harris is trying to make Buescher out to be sexist as well as misogynist. Harris sees no room for opinions other than her own. She is either ignorant or defiant of the Constitution that protects people from this kind of prejudice. Not only is a pro-life person suitable for a judiciary position, but in defending the rights of the unborn, he is particularly suitable. The United States Constitution, the supreme law of America, protects people from the likes of Dianne Feinstein, Kamala Harris, and others. Unfortunately, religious bigotry, especially against Catholics, persists among high ranking politicians whose attitudes are more pharisaical than fair-minded, more prejudicial than prudential.

Chapter 10

Why America Has Shut the Door to Peace

Everyone, seemingly, wants peace. We are made for peace and are discontented when it is missing in our lives. But it is disingenuous to desire an end without desiring the means to that end. The acquisition of money is desirable but not everyone is willing to work to attain that end. To desire an end means desiring, with equal devotion, the means that will bring it about.

When the Beatles chanted, "All we are saying, just give peace a chance," they presumed that peace is a direct object of chance and required no process that would lead to its possession. Peace is rare because what it requires is generally avoided. Particular virtues are needed before peace has any chance of gracing our lives. Simplistic ideas may be appealing, but they are not rewarding.

Justice, too, although universally desired, must overcome divisions that challenge the brotherhood of man, such as prejudice, racism, nationalism, and radically different approaches to morality. Although charity might appear to be unassailable, it sometimes balks at love for the handicapped, the downtrodden, the dispossessed, and one's enemy.

In his *Summa Theologica,* St. Thomas Aquinas explains what is needed to bring peace into a society. "Peace," he writes, "is the *work of justice* indirectly, in so far as justice removes the obstacles to peace; but it is the work of charity directly, since charity, according to its very nature, causes peace" (ST, II-II, q.29, a. 3, ad 3). We can join the Angelic doctor in agreeing that on an interpersonal level, where there is love, there is peace.

To desire peace, therefore, means to desire justice as well as charity. And here is the roadblock to peace. Lawyers and judges swear to uphold the law which includes fighting crimes that work against peace. God-fearing citizens are called to express charity toward their neighbor. But are the virtues of justice and charity being carried out? In his book, *Man and the State*, Jacques Maritain astutely combines justice and charity when he maintains that "Justice is a primary condition for the existence of the body politic, but *Friendship* is its very life-giving form."

In the United States, in the present era, justice and charity have fallen far short of their ideal. Abortion laws are framed so that there is no justice for the unborn. This injustice spreads to people who stand up for justice who are routinely fined, vilified, and, at times, even incarcerated. Saint Teresa of Calcutta has warned that there can be no peace in a society that performs abortions.

At the same time, charity, being associated with religion, is misinterpreted as an unacceptable imposition on others as well as a rejection of human rights. Consequently, over the past two years, hundreds of Catholic Churches have been vandalized, church attendance has significantly declined, while religion, in general has lost its moral authority. The Bible is now politically incorrect. Church leaders do little to ameliorate the situation for fear of being regarded as out-of-date.

For Aquinas, peace is an ultimate value in society. In his *Commentary of St. Matthew*, he makes the following statement: "As life is in a man, so is peace in a kingdom; and as there can be no health

Chapter 10: Why America Has Shut the Door to Peace

without moderation of the humors, so there is peace when a body retains its proper order. And as when health declines, the man verges toward his death, so when peace declines, the kingdom verges toward it death. So that the ultimate thing that must be sought is peace."

Here, Aquinas is building on St. Augustine's definition of peace as "the tranquility of order" and enlarging it to apply to society as a whole. Desire for the ultimate must include a desire for the penultimate. In order to obtain a college diploma, one must take a certain number of courses. If diplomas were handed out like tissues, there would be no education. There can be no peace without justice and charity. Let us first work on these two virtues. If they are realized, then peace will flow spontaneously.

Abortion and racism are clearly divisive. This is to say, they create disorder. And disorder breeds mayhem. Abortion opposes justice for the unborn; racism opposes the brotherhood of man. Both feature radical inequality.

Robert M. Hutchins, former Chancellor of the University of Chicago, has provided a cogent synthesis of peace, charity, and justice in the interest of framing a plan for world peace. In his treatise, *St. Thomas and the World State*, he writes the following: "The work of religion and the church is charity. The work of the state and government is justice. Church and State—universal church and world state—must now work together for world peace founded on universal charity, which would realize the brotherhood of man, and universal democracy, which would bring justice to all mankind."

Hutchins' vision may be more optimistic than realistic, more Pollyannish than political. But his philosophy is sound and it shows us how far away Americans (as well as nations of the world) are at the present moment from achieving peace. As a matter of fact, they have shut the door on peace. There may be peace in the home, where justice and charity preside, but it does reach much further than that. Neighborhoods can be contentious. Americans have closed the door to peace because they have initially closed the door to God who is pre-eminently peace, justice, and charity.

III.

Education

Chapter 11

Dear Old Golden Rule Days

Baseball has rules, as everybody knows. Without them the game could not be played. It would be unintelligible and utterly chaotic. My favorite rule is the "infield fly rule". It states that if there are fewer than two outs and the batter hits an infield fly ball that is deemed by the umpire to be eminently catchable, the batter is automatically out. This is a good rule. It protects the baserunner if the fielder intentionally drops the ball to start a double-play. The rule was established in the interest of fairness. It is, therefore, one that is worthy of having its place. Some rules are welcomed, praised, and accepted because they are reasonable and make perfect sense.

Well, that's baseball, and the reason that it continues to be a fan favorite is because it has integrity. But then there is life in which rules are commonly regarded as restrictions that prevent the full expression of freedom. William Murchison, senior editor of *The Human Life Review*, has observed that "We human beings—we spiritual descendants of Adam and Eve—have been in the rule-smashing business a long time, and are pretty good at it". "There is no list of rules", according to one writer, "There is one rule. The rule is: there are no rules". "Rules and responsibilities," these are the ties that bind us," says another. A ruler cannot rule without the employment of good rules. And he will be judged by how well he uses them. Paradoxically, we use rules to determine which rules are useful and which ones are not.

I recall a young woman proudly declaring that she hates rules and whenever she finds one, she breaks it. She enunciated her sentence, however, without breaking a single rule of grammar. It is hard to avoid rules completely. Rules hold things together. Without rules, everything collapses. The grammarian may be a bore, but his rules of grammar make communication possible.

In the movie *High Society*, Frank Sinatra refrains from taking advantage of the voluptuous Grace Kelly, despite her inebriated state. "There are rules about those things," he says, affirming his good moral sense. Rules defend us. They serve to safeguard our rights and protect our common interests. They can be barriers that keep us out of danger, guideposts they direct our lives.

Rules are ordinances of reason. We should understand that we gain freedom *through* reason, not *from* reason. There are bad rules, certainly. But reason can be summoned to make the distinction between rules that are good and those that are bad. The Golden Rule, however, "do unto others as you would do unto yourself," is unassailable.

Another reason for rejecting rules in general is that they are deemed old fashioned. We may regard "Schooldays, school days, dear old golden rule days," as antiquated, especially when they are "taught to the tune of a hickory stick". Teaching should not be imposing but elucidating. We do not welcome the return of the hickory stick. Yet should we be taught that the fewer rules we have, the more freedom we gain? "In olden days, a glimpse of stocking was seen as something shocking, now heaven knows, anything goes".

But there is a serious problem, when "anything goes" – chaos arrives. Jordan B. Peterson hit the jackpot by telling people that

Chapter 11: Dear Old Golden Rule Days

without rules, their lives are out of order. His "12 Rules for Life," are intended to provide an antidote to the chaos that prevails both in the lives of individuals as well as in the world in general. Some of his rules may be questioned, such as "Pet a cat when you encounter one on the street," but he is to be commended for explaining the essential importance of rules and painting in vivid colors what happens when rules are abandoned.

Mortimer Adler offers 11 rules for analytic reading in his monograph, *How to Read a Book*. His rules, unlike Jordan's 12 rules, do not relate directly to life, but to how to get the most out of reading a book. It may be said, however, that being enriched by a good book can be beneficial to one's life. The author does point out that his modest effort relates to "life, liberty, and the pursuit of happiness".

Scripture tells us how we behave in the absence of rules. We involve ourselves in things that are beneath us. While Moses was away, the rule-less Hebrews danced around a Golden Calf. Moses returned to restore order by bringing into their lives, the Ten Commandments, which are also ten essential rules for living with God in mind and with a sense of dignity in one's soul. God loves rules because are consistent with His love for human beings who are created in his image.

Do we want to return to the "dear old golden rule days? We cannot turn back the clock, but we might bring forward some of the good rules of the past. We still need courtesy, respect, and the civility to say "please" and "thank you" even when we are being suffocated by unnecessary bureaucratic rules.

We should not abandon rules because we think they are old fashioned, frivolous, foolish, and opposed to freedom. Paradoxically, we should welcome them as long as they provide guidance, balance, propriety, and proper restraint. We cannot rule our own lives unless we honor the rules that make it possible.

Chapter 12

Manipulating Words
For the Purpose of Manipulating Minds

According to The Oxford Dictionary, to manipulate is "to control or influence (a person or situation) cleverly, unfairly, or unscrupulously". It is the antithesis of "to inform" which respects the integrity of the person to whom one is speaking. A person, then, has a right not to be manipulated. A synonym for manipulating a person is "exploitation," which has aroused a strong sense of indignation in the modern world.

The push for euthanasia in Canada is made clear by the deceptive use of words intended to make attractive the notion of putting people to death. The manipulation of six words in particular warrant close attention, for they dishonor human freedom. They are: dignity, discrimination, treatment, MAiD, dying, and euthanasia.

An application filed by Dying with Dignity in Ontario superior court contends that it is "discriminatory" to bar people with mental disorders from being eligible for an assisted death which it is available to people who suffer physically. The term "dignity" is manipulated to create the false impression that being put to death is somehow more dignified than a death that results from an illness. Dignity has a twofold meaning. On the one hand it refers to the innate dignity of a human being which cannot be removed. No matter how a person dies, his intrinsic dignity remains intact. In this sense, everyone dies with dignity. The second meaning is socio/cultural. Certain awkward or embarrassing acts, that we need not specify, may appear to be undignified. Dying while being connected to a machine and various apparatuses may be cumbersome and unwieldy, but it is not undignified. Being put to death does not create a dignity that was not present previously.

The word "discriminate" is the most manipulated word in the English language. To discriminate simply means to make a distinction: this is a dog and that is a cat. To discriminate in this sense means to engage in the act of thinking. This original meaning of the word is almost completely overshadowed by a form of discrimination that is unjust. The Dying with Dignity lobby group distinguishes between those who are eligible for assisted death who suffer physically and those who suffer mentally. And then it leaps to the conclusion that the latter group is unjustly discriminated against because it is not treated equally with the former group. One might as well say that it is discriminatory to withhold euthanasia from people who are in perfect health. But not all forms of discrimination lead to unjust discrimination. To discriminate between the sick and the healthy does not infer that they should be treated equally.

A Canadian Forces veteran sought treatment for post-traumatic stress disorder (PTSD) and a traumatic brain injury. He was shocked when he was unexpectedly and casually, offered medical assistance in dying by a Veterans affairs Canada employee. In time, he discovered that several others veterans were also offered euthanasia as a "treatment" option of PTSD. The word "treatment" refers to a form of caring for a patient with the hope of improving his condition. It must be stretched beyond its original meaning to include putting a person to death. Then it ceases to be a treatment but a finality.

Chapter 12: Manipulating Words

The term MAiD (Medical assistance in dying) is both an acronym and a euphemism for a female servant. In reality, it represents the grim reaper. In addition, such assistance is not to "help" a person to die, but to hasten his death by killing him. A person's demise is far too important to be misrepresented as some form of assistance.

Finally, the covering term, "euthanasia," which is derived from the Greek meaning "beautiful death," is not exactly beautiful. In many reported cases, it is painful and therefore, not at all beautiful.

Twisting language out of shape in order to exploit people is unconscionable. Words can be as lethal as bullets. We should expect more linguistic integrity from the medical profession. As it stands, many of them need to be treated for semantic aphasia. Education should inculcate a profound respect for the word.

Former Secretary-General of the United Nations, Dag Hammarskjöld, reminds us by his own eloquent employment of words, how they must engender respect. "*Respect for the word* is the first commandment in the discipline by which a man can be educated to maturity—intellectual emotional, and moral. *Respect for the word*--to employ it with scrupulous care and an incorruptible love of truth—is essential if there is to be any growth in society or in the human race. To misuse the word is to show contempt for man. It undermines the bridges and poisons the wells. It causes Man to regress down the long path of his evolution" (*Markings*).

Alexander Solzhenitsyn averred that he studied words in his dictionary "as if they were precious stones, each so precious that I would not exchange one for another".

The manipulation of words for the purpose of manipulation of minds is the perfect opposite of what we should expect from the medical profession or the government. The manipulator begins with a questionable end he has in mind. He knows that honesty will not serve his purposes, so he manipulates words and teases people, without their realizing it, to work for his end. History teaches how common this practice is, but new words undergo new transformations and past iniquities continue to repeat themselves. Words are meant to serve the truth, but they often serve the lie.

Let us heed the words of Socrates: "False words are not only evil in themselves, but they infect the soul with evil."

Chapter 13

Surprising Facts We Should Know about Fetal Development

As we become absorbed by the business of life, we are distracted from the wonder of life. We are often distracted from who we really are. There are times when activity must yield to meditation. How can a single cell, in biological terms called a zygote, continue to divide until there are 28 trillion of them in the 10-year-old child, all finding their right place, and all cooperating with each other to form a complete and unified organism? And what is more, this organism is endowed with consciousness and a sense of right and wrong.

Katrina Furth has a PhD in Neuroscience and specializes in communicating science concepts with non-scientific audiences. She has worked as an adjunct professor at Catholic university in Washington, DC. Her meticulous scholarship has led her to the irresistible conclusion that "The wonder of fetal development points like a spotlight to a gifted Creator in Heaven."

The Greek philosopher, Heraclitus, offered the world the often repeated epigram, "Nature loves to hide". The correlative should be, "Humans love to seek." There is a fascinating connection between concealment and discovery. We may also state that the author of nature also loves to hide and invites us to discover His presence in a thousand different ways. Dr. Kurth employs the word "spotlight" to indicate how evidence can shed light, even illuminate the reality of its Author.

In his *History of Animals,* Book 6, part 3, Aristotle describes the first appearance of the heart as *punctum saliens* (leaping point). Since then, our knowledge of the heart has grown to be encyclopedic.

The heart is the first organ to function in the development of the fetus. It begins to beat at 6 weeks gestation. After that, the fetal heart outpaces the mother's heart. The adult heart, on average, beats from 60 to 100 times per minute. The fetal heart beats 170 times per minute at ten weeks gestation and throughout its period in the womb will beat 54 million times. To understand how remarkable this is, we can resort to a simple experiment. Let us mimic the beating heart by bringing our fingers to the palm of the hand in a rapid fashion. When we repeat this motion for two minutes or so, our hand grows weary. We could not continue this exercise for very long. Yet the heart, whether in the fetus or in the adult, continues to beat indefinitely and without tiring.

Ultrasound imaging of the fetal heart reveals the rhythmic propulsion of life-sustaining blood coursing through the body. The "Heartbeat Law" in South Carolina restricts abortion to six weeks after the heart has begun to beat. The law states that abortions cannot be performed after an ultrasound has detected "cardiac activity or the steady and repetitive rhythmic contraction of the fetal heart, within the gestational sac." In this case, the heart is seen as an indication that the fetus is human and has the right to go on living. Nonetheless, the fetus prior to six weeks is an integral part of the fetus throughout its gestation. Six weeks does mark the end of the "pre-fetus" and the beginning of the fetus as human. All that precedes the 6-week fetus is just as remarkable as what ensues. The fetus, throughout its term, cannot be divided into human and non-human.

The formation of the brain begins in the fifth week of gestation as a three-millimeter-long neural tube. The upper regions of the neural tube expand and fold to create the recognizable brain. By five and a half months or so, the brain takes on its adult shape. Billions of threadlike fibers crisscross the brain, forming labyrinthine networks that relay messages between different brain regions. Each sensory system develops in an interactive way. It is during the prenatal period that the brain undergoes its greatest growth.

It is interesting to note that the fetus has almost 100 more bones than the adult. The adult has 206 bones whereas prior to birth the fetus has between 275 and 300 bones. These additional bones fuse together to form larger bones. In so many ways, the unborn outpaces his future self.

Fetal development proceeds independently of fetal intelligence. Yet it is naïve to think that it simply develops naturally. In his fifth proof for the existence of God, St. Thomas Aquinas makes the following statement: "Now whatever lacks intelligence cannot move towards an end, unless it be directed by some being endowed with knowledge and intelligence; as the arrow is shot to its mark by the archer. Therefore some intelligent being exists by whom all natural things are directed to their end; and this being we call God" (*Summa Theologica*, I, 2, 3).

The development of the fetus, which involves billions upon billions of intricate and interacting factors, is of such an order of complexity that it clearly exceeds anything that human beings have ever accomplished using their own intelligence and knowledge. This fact is a powerful and convincing argument for the existence of an omnipotent architect. Fetal development does not take place on its own. Nor is, or could it be, the accomplishment of human ingenuity.

To cite Dr. Kurth once more in closing, "From its inception when sperm and egg fuse in the pinnacle of adulthood, human life develops according to the intricate craftsmanship of a divine Creator" (*The Human Life Review*, Summer/Fall 20024, p. 35).

Chapter 14

Darwin's Dark Deprivation

Charles Darwin's *Origin of the Species by Natural Selection* (1859) is a sustained treatment of how the diversity of organisms came about as the result of natural processes. "It is not the strongest of the species that survives," he wrote, "not the most intelligent that survives. It is the one that is the most adaptable to change." The causes of these changes would be external, largely environmental or random. He was successful in explaining certain changes in finch beaks, horse hoofs, and moth coloration. But he was unable to explain the origin of any species.

Darwin labored under a great handicap inasmuch as he knew nothing of biochemistry which holds the key to understanding any kind of evolutionary process. He did not have the benefit, for example, of electron microscopy which revealed subcellular structures. The rock bottom factors of life were simply not available to him. As early as 1871, 'natural selection' seemed to be a woefully incomplete explanation for changes in species. One of Darwin's critics in that year, by the name of St. George Mivart, remarked that "there are many remarkable phenomena in organic forms upon which 'natural selection' throws no light whatsoever." Darwin's theory had limited application and related to what is called "gross anatomy" rather than to the origin of the species. From the perspective of the contemporary world, Darwin's efforts were severely deprived.

In his *Origin of the Species*, Darwin states the following: "If it could be demonstrated that any complex organ existed which could not possibly have been formed by numerous, successive, slight modifications, my theory would absolutely break down." This is an honest admission on the part of the distinguished scientist."

If Darwin had the privilege of knowing how a single cell zygote evolves to produce a splendidly functioning ten-year-old child, let us say, he would have been astonished and would have agreed whole heartedly about the extreme limitations of his theory. What would he think if he could look inside of a subject instead of outside?

Let us imagine a superhuman biologist who possessed the uncanny ability to place a new cell every second in the right place and at the right time in the development of the human being. Let us also imagine that our super-biologist would work constantly and indefatigably without eating or sleeping. How far would he get if he were given an endless amount of time? Over the course of a year, there are 31 million, 449 thousand, and 600 seconds. After 1,000 years the number of seconds would attain the staggering figure of 31 billion, 449, million, and 600 thousand. At this point after deftly working for 100 billion years, our super-biologist would be less than 10% on his way to spending the 72 trillion 576 billion years it would take to match the number of cells in the typical ten-year-old boy.

Can we suggest that this prodigality of nature cannot possibly be explained by Darwinian thinking? In fact, it is perfectly reasonable to suggest that it is the work of a Divine Architect. One of the reasons that Darwinian evolution became immensely popular was because it intimated that if species came about as a result of chance, then God was not in the picture. This is why Lynn Margulis, a Distinguished University Professor of Biology at the University of Mas-

Chapter 14: Darwin's Dark Deprivation

sachusetts regards Darwinism as "a minor twentieth century religious sect within the sprawling persuasion of Anglo-Saxon biology . . . Neo-Darwinism, which insists on (the slow accrual of mutations is in a complete funk" and Notre Dame University professor Peter van Ingwan refers to Darwinism being "more as an ideology than as a scientific theory."

Biochemistry has made quantum leaps since 1859 which have superannuated Darwinism. From a modern point of view, Darwin was literally working in the dark. In his highly insightful work, *Darwin's Black Box,* Michael Behe remarks that there are "mountains and chasms that block a Darwinian explanation of life."

To suggest that God is involved in the creation and development of life is not to demean science. No one is opposed to science marching on and discovering more and more about the nature of the physical world. At the same time, we must recognize that science has its limitations. We look with wonder at the organization of the universe and our mind is overwhelmed. Philosophy has its legitimate place. The most incomprehensive thing about the universe, to cite Albert Einstein, is the fact that it is comprehensible. The answer to how this attunement that the mind has with reality came about is something that exists outside the province of science. Science should not claim to be omnivorous.

Let us consider the words of one of the most endeared among philosophers, Socrates of Athens: "Is it not to be admired . . . that the mouth through which the food is conveyed should be placed so near the nose and eyes as to prevent the passage unnoticed of whatever is unfit for nourishment? And canst thou still doubt, Aristodemus, whether a disposition of parts like this should be the work of chance, or of wisdom and contrivance." St. Thomas Aquinas speaks more simply and directly in his *Summa Theologica* when states that "We see that things which lack knowledge, such as natural bodies, act for an end, and this is evident from their acting always, or nearly always, in the same way, so as to obtain the best result. Hence it is plain that they achieve their end not fortuitously, but designedly."

Darwinism today is truly an ideology. God, the Great Designer, is and always is, a reality.

Chapter 15

On the Subject of Miracles

Are Miracles Possible?

Science, which studies the nature and order of the physical universe, by virtue of its limitations, is unable to confirm or deny that there are such things as miracles. A miracle, by definition, defies the laws of nature. Being habituated to what science can reveal, people tend to take a skeptical view of miracles. Thus, John Henry Cardinal Newman can state, in his book, Essays on Miracles, that a miracle is "an event in a given system which cannot be referred to any law, or accounted for by the operation of any principle, in that system".

The now canonized Saint John Henry Newman is not denying the possibility of miracles, but merely pointing out that science cannot prove their existence. There are many windows through which we can ascertain reality; science is just one of them. Many scientists readily admit how limited their knowledge really is. The distinguished astronomer, Robert Jastrow, who believed that the Big Bang Theory left room for the existence of God, ended one of his books by stating that the scientist, "who has lived by his faith in the power of reason . . . has scaled the mountains of ignorance . . . he is about to conquer the highest peak; [as] he pulls himself over the final rock, he is greeted by a band or theologians who have been sitting there for centuries". There are more things going on in heaven and earth that we can divine by reason alone. Science has not told us the whole story. In the words of another astronomer, Carl Sagan, "science is a way of thinking much more than it a body of knowledge

Are Miracles Plausible?

Both the Old and New Testaments are replete with references to miracles. Newman points out that "the pure morality of the gospel, as taught by illiterate fishermen of Galilee," must be considered to be miraculous. He also contends that the rapid expanse of Christianity under social circumstances extremely hostile to it, must also be considered miraculous. Miracles are plausible because they happen. Evangelist Leonard Ravenhill (1907-1994) holds that, "The greatest miracle that God can do today is to take an unholy man out of an unholy world and make him holy, then put him back into that unholy world and keep him holy in it." In this context, we might think of the Confessions of St. Augustine.

It was the Bishop of Hippo who also declared that "all things are miraculous". Here Augustine is alluding to another area that is closed to the scientist, namely, how did things come about in the first place? Scientists take it for granted that there is a universe that happens to be ordered. But they are helpless in determining its origin. Hence, its very origin and the very existence of everything that it contains is also miraculous. As the American essayist, Ralph Waldo Emerson has stated, "The invariable mark of wisdom is to see the miraculous in the common".

Miracles are plausible because there is a God who is all-powerful. Miracles do not make any sense to the atheist who sees nothing more than what his reason can discern. Miracles cannot crop up all by themselves. They need an agency that superintends the universe and displays His creative powers in diverse ways. From God's point of view, a miracle is just another way of speaking to His human creatures.

Are Miracles Purposeful?

Christ's miracles always have a moral purpose. They are avenues of love which are more convincingly miraculous because of their immediacy. Medicine is imperfect and usually requires a period for healing to take place. Christ's healing miracles are startling and stand apart from healing measures that are purely natural.

Another purpose associated with His miracles is to provide evidence that there is a God, and one who cares about his creatures. The possibility of miracles provides a motivation for prayer. That possibility is also an incentive to develop and exercise one's native abilities. The distinguished novelist, Vladimir Nabokov (1899-1977) saw his art as a call to fulfill his natural talent: "The pages are still blank, but there is a miraculous feeling of the words being there, written in invisible ink and clamoring to become visible".

Mother Angelica famously stated that "Unless you are willing to do the ridiculous, God will not do the miraculous". For the esteemed nun, these words were more than an empty phrase; they encapsulated her life. Miracles can be answers to prayers, to hard work for a good cause, or to reveal the majesty of God. They are purposeful but never gratuitous. The miracle at Cana, Christ's first miracle, was public and performed at the request of his mother. Christ transformed approximately 120 gallons of water into wine, the quality of which was highly praised by the host. The overriding meaning of the miracle is to emphasize the sanctity of marriage. The significance of this miracle has continuing significance for every marriage. In a comparable miracle, Narcissus, the Bishop of Jerusalem (first century), when oil failed for the lamps on the vigil of Easter, sent for water. When the water arrived, he prayed over it, and it changed to serviceable oil. The Bishop was a holy man and lived to the remarkable age of a hundred and sixteen, or more, according to Eusebius. Miracles are possible, plausible, and purposeful. We begin our appreciation of miracles by regarding our own existence as a miracle.

IV.

Philosophy

Chapter 16

Philosophy, Osmosis and Abortion

Philosophy is the active pursuit of truth. It is not a haphazard collection of ideas. Nor is it the uncritical acceptance of someone else's set of ideas. Philosophy presupposes two virtues that are rarely combined in the same person: a modesty, untainted by the ego, which is open to the unvarnished truth of things, and the courage to stand by truth no matter how unpopular it may be. A true philosopher does not croak under the weight of criticism.

Throughout history, opposition to abortion was largely cultural. It was generally accepted that abortion was the killing of a developing human being and therefore disgraceful. Philosophy was not needed to arrive at this common sense conclusion. As culture maverick Jordan Peterson has stated the matter, simply and forthrightly, "Abortion is clearly wrong". The moral atmosphere in today's culture, however, has shifted dramatically. It is no longer united in its opposition to abortion. In fact, it rails against those who oppose abortion. A sound philosophy, therefore, is now needed more than ever to awaken people to exactly what abortion is and to the adverse effects it has brought to both the family and society.

Unfortunately, philosophy has become a joke. To quote Bill Maher, "philosophy is as useful as a bidet in a gorilla cage". Cynics have referred to the philosopher as "a blind man in a dark cellar at midnight looking for a black cat that isn't there". This negative attitude toward philosophy even shows up in cartoons. Mell Lazarus, creator of *Miss* Peach, has one youngster speak of philosophy as "thinking about all the problems facing humanity and how troubled the world is". "That must be a dumb philosophy of life", snaps a classmate. "My philosophy of life is 'Don't Think'." The noble pursuit of truth has been replaced, by and large, by relativism in which abortion and birth depend on one's perspective and therefore are neither right nor wrong in themselves. And if not relativism, then deconstructionism or nihilism that erase all meaning. In short, philosophy is rejected because it is said to be medieval.

If the philosopher is searching for truth, he is also looking for hope. The expression "abortion without apology" implies "abortion without thinking". But man is essentially a thinking thing and the embarrassing realization that he is not thinking may inspire his return to thinking in a philosophical manner. If the typical defender of abortion is not thinking, he is, we might say, getting his ideas through osmosis. That could be a rather humiliating revelation.

Osmosis, as anyone who has taken a high school course in biology knows, is the tendency of a fluid, usually water, to pass through a semipermeable membrane into a solution where the solvent concentration is higher, thus equalizing the concentrations of materials on either side of the membrane. The term "osmosis" is a Latinized form of the Greek word, *osmos*, meaning "a push". It also refers to the gradual or unconscious assimilation of ideas.

Education, in the truest sense, is a conscious assimilation of ideas that conform to reality. It is a process by which objective data passes through the senses and are possessed by the knower. Education is not the same as osmosis, although what passes for education in many instances these days is often the passage of toxic cultural ideas

Chapter 16: Philosophy, Osmosis and Abortion

through a weak defense system into a susceptible person, thus forming a mirror image of culture. In other words, the osmotic process in education is akin to extreme socialization or acculturation in which both the mind and culture have an equal concentration of the same ideas.

When Dostoevsky submitted his manuscript, *Crime and Punishment*, to the publisher, he included a note stating that his story was about a university student whose mind was infected by incomplete ideas that float on the wind. The Great Russian novelist understood that education is not the same as infection. Raskolnikov, the main character of the book, did not understand his culture because he was possessed by it.

Dostoevsky's use of the word "incomplete" is a marvelous example of restraint. The ideas of the protagonist were not, in the author's mind, stupid, nonsensical, or foolish. They were "incomplete". This means that they did have something positive about them, but they simply lacked something more that would give them a certain completeness. Abortion can be attractive because it is a "choice" which is a valued capacity in the human being. But this idea is woefully incomplete because it ignores that which is chosen, which, as in the case of Raskolnikov, was murder. Abortion is seen as an act of freedom. Yet, freedom of choice is morally incomplete if it is not linked to freedom of fulfillment. The very meaning of freedom of choice is to align that freedom to a higher freedom, freedom of fulfillment. Furthermore, the unborn is not part of the woman's body. A more complete understanding indicates that it is located in her body but has a destiny of its own. Most abortions are done for convenience. The virtue of convenience is that it saves time. But it does not specify the total loss of time for the unborn child. Finally, a woman does not have a "right" to abort, but only the possibility. But it is a possibility that does not rise to the dignity of a right.

The rhetoric for the abortion advocate is incomplete. It is like half a loaf. But the willingness to remain incomplete is to prefer the half-loaf to the full one. If there could ever be a genuine dialogue on the issue of abortion, it would consist of pro-lifers encouraging abortion advocates to make their thinking complete. It is like saying, "Good, you are on second base, now come home". That should be more effective than saying, "you are completely wrong!" Truth does not make comprises. Being half right is still being wrong. Nonetheless, it is a stepping stone. And, as Confucius has said, "It does not matter how slowly you go, as long as you do not stop".

Saint Thomas Aquinas understood the osmotic process by which people are infected by incomplete cultural ideas in moral terms: "There is not much sinning because of man's natural desires. But the stimuli of desire which man's cunning has devised are something else, and for the sake of these one sins very much." The Angelic Philosopher is being positive in referring to our nature as being essentially good. But if our nature is good, we should use it well. We are immersed in culture and are sitting ducks for the various temptations it provides. A person becomes more inclined to sin through cultural seduction than because of his natural appetites. Aquinas' statement is sympathetic toward vulnerable human beings and sharply critical of the concentration of bad ideas that circulate within culture.

The distinguished Thomistic philosopher, Josef Pieper is agreement with Saint Thomas. In his classic, *The Four Cardinal Virtues*,

Chapter 16: Philosophy, Osmosis and Abortion

he states that "Intemperance is enkindled above all by the seductive glamour of the stimuli provided in an artificial civilization, with which the dishonorable team of blind lust and calculated greed surround the province of sexuality". This is a bombshell of a sentence! Temperance is one of the four cardinal virtues. Lust and greed are two of the seven deadly sins. The combination of intemperance with two deadly sins is explosive. We need strong virtues in order to resist the lure of a synthesis of strong temptations.

St. Thomas uses the term "cunning". Since the 13th century this notion has become greatly enlarged and is now accurately expressed in the modern era by the phrase that Pieper employs: "artificial civilization". Technology dominates the cultural landscape and along with it, pornography, abortion, euthanasia, gender dysphoria, puberty blockers, and harmful drugs, together with various "devices" that hyper-stimulate. Our weak "semipermeable membrane" is a poor defense against the toxic ideas that "push" their way into our hearts and minds.

The daily news informs us of the pandemic of moral horrors, including mass murders, which have left many people both confused and distraught. The attempt to rectify the situation seems futile as the problems increase. The essence of the moral problems that are currently tearing society apart is something that is usually ignored. Furthermore, the application of the usual bromides, especially those of a political nature, is insufficient. One must go to the heart of the dilemma.

On one side of the problem is a seductive culture. Yet, the liberal mood in society (which is to say, freedom without responsibility) that has helped to bring about this plague of problems remains unattended. Nonetheless, something must be done to begin the detoxification of culture. The first step would be to awaken people to the fact that the great liberal experiment has not only failed but has worsened the situation.

On the other side of the problem is the relatively defenseless person, especially the teenager whose moral defense system has not been adequately developed, who is a victim of today's artificial world. The remedies for this problem are more within reach than the task of transforming culture. Families and small communities must take the initiative and instruct people about the present situation which demands understanding, discipline, the development of one's spirituality, and community support. If people are freezing within their house, the solution is not to add clothing but to get at the source of the problem which is the open door that is inviting the cold.

We baptize a bad culture with the word "progress". G. K. Chesterton has reminded us, however, that "progress is a comparative about which we have not settled the superlative". Where are we going? At the same time, we boast that we are "liberal". Unfortunately, we are not at all happy with what is going on. The Danish poet, Piet Hien, has remarked that "The noble art of losing face may one day save the human race". Recognizing that being "liberal" is not liberating requires "losing face". We must abandon the twin illusions that we are experiencing cultural progress and that liberal politics is a corrective for all out ills. Character, so badly needed, is built not through osmosis but through the combination learning, discipline, brotherly love, and God's readily available assistance.

Chapter 16: Philosophy, Osmosis and Abortion

Philosophy has much to say about abortion. But it also sheds light on the climate that seduces people into thinking that abortion is a good. Dostoevsky, Pieper, and Aquinas belong to different centuries. They speak in different languages and write in radically different forms. The more important point is that they all attest to the universality of philosophy. They urge their readers to think realistically and resist the lure of the world. Marshall McLuhan, who directed his philosophical abilities to understanding the media, informs us that, "When the human spirit feels drawn into the mesh of the man-made images of the electric world, it sacrifices its identity". Narcissus spent his last days transfixed by his own image mirrored in the pool. By looking at himself, he could see nothing else. Narcissism and abortion are curiously intertwined.

The purpose of philosophy is understanding. This is fundamental in the sense that it serves as the basis for all the positive things that follow. Without a basis, the edifice crumbles. Nonetheless, philosophy is not enough. Added to understanding must be warmth and acceptance. To be pro-life is to be part of a community that is broad enough to encompass everyone. We the living must share our lives with everyone, as much as possible, including, of course, our enemies. Life is to be shared. Abortion sets itself against this sharing of life. Therefore, it represents a moral problem which cannot be ignored. Words can enlighten. Love can accept. We live by a hope that is not discouraged by difficulty. Each human life is of infinite importance. How much good each of us can accomplish in our brief hour is known only to God. But we find joy and meaning as we never cease striving.

Chapter 17

The Paradox of the Human Being

The words "know thyself" were chiseled over the entrance of the temple at Delphi. The original meaning of these words advises man to "Enter into yourself; allow yourself to be told by God that you are only a human being". Thus, anyone entering the temple would lower his voice out of humility. The Roman poet, Juvenal, believed these words, so profound in their significance, came from heaven. "O God," exclaimed St. Augustine, "I pray you let me know myself". Socrates exemplified the spirit of these words, when he announced to his disciples that the unexamined life is not worth living. It is not an easy thing to know oneself. Nonetheless, that knowledge is essential for the human being to be himself.

Being told that one is "only a human being" need not be discouraging. On the one hand it warns against attempting to be more than a human being. We find this vain attempt with Adam in the Garden of Eden, with the fictional Prometheus, and with Friedrich Nietzsche's "Superman". We also find it in anyone who presumes to have an authority that belongs exclusively to God. It was appropriate, therefore, that beside those two words was the maxim, "Nothing in excess".

On the other hand, "know thyself" directs man to look into himself and discover the great potential that is his birthright. The human being is greater than he realizes, but not greater than his nature will allow. His greatness must be tempered. We cannot be what we are not, yet what we can be makes life worth living. That inward treasure has been brought to light by the great personalities of history. We think of the extraordinary accomplishments of Aquinas, Dante, Bach, Michelangelo, Da Vinci, Shakespeare, Pope John Paul II, and others, and recognize what a great gift it is to be a human being.

Gabriel Marcel, who is a modern Socratic, states the following in his book, *Les hommes contre l'humain*: "I had a remarkable experience recently. I was coming home from a concert where I heard Bach played and I experienced in myself a revival of a feeling or rather of a certainty that seems to have been lost in our time: the honor of being human".

We need forms of beauty to remind us of the dignity of being human. Mozart is a fellow human being and communicates, for our edification, a transcendent message that immediately informs us that a human being is a truly extraordinary creature. If a human being can do this, we say to ourselves, a human being has reserves that make him truly special. It is in this vein that the philosopher Nikolai Berdyaev exclaims that beauty will save the world.

For many, however, this glorious creature fails to realize who he is. He detests himself, as Pascal states. He is a robber, a villain, a traitor, a tyrant, a murderer. And yet, as Gerard Manley Hopkins has written, "This Jack, joke, poor potsherd, patch, matchwood, immortal diamond; Is immortal diamond". He is an immortal diamond who belongs to God.

Hamlet's tragedy lay in the fact that he had lost the enjoyment of being human. The world had become, for him, entirely without interest. What was once exhilarating fresh air had become, for him, "nothing … but a foul and pestilent congregation of vapours". And yet, he still recognized the greatness of man: "What a piece of work

Chapter 17: The Paradox of the Human Being

is a man! How Noble in reason! How infinite in faculty! In form and moving how express and admirable! In Action, how like an Angel in apprehension, how like a God! The beauty of the world, the paragon of animals—and yet, to me, what is this quintessence of dust?"

Hamlet is divided. The dignity of his humanity is lost in the misery that he experiences. He knows that he is the "quintessence of dust" but cannot experience that lofty status. In a sense, Hamlet is Everyman since he fails to live up to what is most noble in his being.

When the Psalmist declares, "What is man that God is mindful of him?" (Psalm 8), he brings to mind the notion that man may be unworthy of His love. "O the grandeur and the littleness," cries Pascal, "the excellence and the corruption, the majesty and the meanness, of man". Man is but a speck in an infinite universe. Thomas Carlyle expressed this notion quite eloquently: "When I have gazed into these stars, have they not looked down upon me as if with pity from their serene spaces, like eyes glistening with heavenly tears over the little lot of man?" And yet, man is created in the image and likeness of God.

Christianity, without discarding any of the wisdom of the ancient Greeks, views the glory of man in terms of dying to one's self in order to be born again in Christ. The distinguished theologian Hans Urs von Balthasar has stated that "Human beings were created not to be satisfied with themselves but that, dead to self, they might, in Christ's possession, possess all things in him". To live in Christ overcomes the nettling paradoxes that look at the human being as little, yet great, a finite nature tending toward transcendence, a self who must die to self, and a creature unworthy of love, and yet loved.

Christ reveals man to himself. He dispels the confusion in the embrace of divine Love.

Chapter 18

A Note on the Supreme Wisdom

Wisdom is not only difficult to achieve, but difficult to express. Undertaking the latter, however, is worthwhile since it may serve as a stepping stone to its achievement.

We begin with a notion that is easy to apprehend. There are two fundamental things we can say about anything that exists. First of all, that it is something: a human being, a dog, a tree, or a flower. Philosophers use the word *essence* to refer to all these things that exist. Essence answers the question, "what is it"? A human being has the essence of a human being, a dog, the essence of a dog, and so on. The second thing we can say about anything that exists is that it *exists*. That is, it stands outside of nothingness. All the things in the universe have both an *essence* and an *existence*. These two fundamental features are combined to give reality to any particular kind of thing. We are all essences who exist.

While it is easy to understand the notion of *essence*, the notion of *existence* eludes us. Although every being is composed of an essence and an existence, the latter is shrouded in mystery. This is because *existence* does not exist. Now, that is a startling statement! The truth of the matter is that we cannot have a concept of existence. We cannot draw a picture of *existence*, though we know without any doubt that it is real. Trying to think of existence all by itself is akin to trying to hear the sound of one hand clapping.

Science is the study of essences. It studies everything from atoms to galaxies, from the one-celled protozoan to the multi-trillion celled human being. But it cannot turn its attention to *existence*. Once it isolates existence from essence, it becomes tongue-tied. It cannot explain why any particular essence came to be or why it exists at all. It is left to philosophy and theology to deal with the mystery of *existence*.

The distinguished astronomer, Sir Arthur Eddington, was the first to confirm Einstein's "Theory of Relativity". He has complained, however, "that philosophers do nothing to make clear to 'laymen' what the word 'existence' means". The reason for this is the fact that the concept of existence surpasses our capacity to understand, let alone make clear. It is something both real and unintelligible. Gottfried Leibniz' enduring question, "Why is there something rather than nothing?" cannot be answered by scientists for it involves existence which is shrouded in mystery.

It is in the Old Testament that we find the first reference to existence itself, separated from essence. Moses did not know the name of God, but he knew that the Jews would ask him for it. In speaking to God he said, "Lo, I shall go to the children of Israel, and say to them: The God of your fathers hath sent me to you. If they should say to me: what is His name? What should I say to them? And God said to Moses: I AM WHO AM: "Thus shalt thou say to the children of Israel: HE WHO IS, hath sent me to you".

God, therefore, is the "being who is". God's essence, unlike any other essence, is *to be*. And since His essence is to be, He must be eternal. This is an epoch-making statement concerning God and how He is distinct from all His creation in an absolute way. Furthermore, it is because God's existence contributes to that of our own,

Chapter 18: A Note on the Supreme Wisdom

according to St. Thomas Aquinas, that "all knowing beings implicitly know God in any and every thing that they know." We are united to God--existence to existence—and that is why we have, in some obscure way an innate sense of His Being. Since no one can account for his own existence, all things point to the fact that there must be a point where essence and existence coincide. And this point is the being WHO IS.

This theologically based notion of God preceded its philosophical correlative expressed in great detail by St. Thomas Aquinas. As a consequence, a harmony exists between theology and philosophy, faith and reason, nature and grace. As Etienne Gilson states in his book, *God and Philosophy*, "He who is the God of the philosophers is HE WHO IS, the God of Abraham, of Isaac, and of Jacob".

Here is the supreme wisdom: to know that God exists, but not knowing His essence, or how we can imagine Him. Accordingly, Gilson states, in his book, *The Spirit of Thomism,* "To understand this supreme truth is to know that we do not know what God is; and to know that, is also to reach the summit of human knowledge in this life".

To think of God as the being Who Is represents the summit of human wisdom. It combines an affirmation of man's philosophical powers with the humility to know God as unknown.

And now, dear reader, I present to you in a single sentence drawn from Jacques Maritain's book, *Existence and the Existent,* a challenge to your philosophical ability and a precise summary of everything stated above: "Why should it be astonishing that at the summit of all beings, at the point where everything is carried to pure transcendent act, the intelligibility of essence should fuse in an absolute identity with the super-intelligibility of existence, both infinitely overflowing what is designated here below by their concepts, in the incomprehensible unity of *Him Who is*?"

Chapter 19

The Wisdom of Knowing When to Stop

Johann Wolfgang von Goethe's *Sorcerer's Apprentice* has an important message for today's society in which, in many crucial areas, people do not know when to stop. In the story, an elderly sorcerer leaves his workshop and entrusts his apprentice with chores to perform. Tired of fetching water by pail, he enchants a broom to do the work for him using magic for which he is not sufficiently trained. Although he can start the process, he cannot stop it. Soon the entire room is filled with water. "The spirits I invoked," states Goethe, "I cannot banish anymore" (*Die Geister, die ich rief, die werd ich nicht mehr los*).

Every automobile is equipped with both a gas pedal and brakes. A car would be a menace if there were no means to stop it once it is moving. This is simply a matter of common sense. On the level of morality, however, common sense does not always prevail.

Not knowing when to stop is a systemic problems for people who are enchanted by the current liberal ideology. Freedom is fine as far as it goes. But it must not go too far. It must, at some point, be restrained. Liberals hail 'freedom," but "restraint" is seldom if ever on their lips.

Abraham Lincoln tells the story of the farmer who said that he was not greedy about land. He wanted only the land that joined his. As a matter of fact, there were not brakes on his greed. King Midas was greedy about gold and gained the privilege of turning everything he touched into that precious metal. As we know from the tale, his unusual gift backfired when he accidentally turned his daughter into gold.

From an historical perspective, abortion has gone through several stages of freedom. It moved from being universally illegal to being permissible in cases of rape or incest. Freedom then spread to when it threatened a woman's life, and then stretched to include her health. But "health" was ambiguous, and abortion was subsequently set under the umbrella of "choice". In the current language of liberalism, abortion should be entirely free of all restrictions. Those who oppose abortion suffer as unchecked freedom continues to advance. Because abortion is now deemed to be a "right," its opponents are cast as criminals and, in some cases, incarcerated for their beliefs. Where, one might ask, does such unleashed freedom stop? It is omnivorous. It echoes the plight of the sorcerer's apprentice who cannot stop what he started.

In order to keep steamrolling, abortion advocates must ignore red lights, the most important of which is the sanctity of life. We should know when to stop at the moment the sanctity of life is in danger.

When the same unbridled freedom is applied to marriage, a succession of arrangements is approved including "open" marriage, same-sex marriage, polyandry, and various forms of promiscuity. The LGBTQ++ consortium is formed in which traditional marriage is downgraded to something akin to entrapment or even slavery. The natural law no longer serves as a red light, nor does the appearance of numerous social diseases. We find a similar trend that approves marijuana and psychedelic drugs.

Chapter 19: The Wisdom of Knowing When to Stop

In a November 6, 2024 article in the *Toronto Star,* columnist Vinay Menon states that president-elect Donald Trump "is a man unshackled." Mr. Menon, however, may be pinning this label on the wrong party. Abortion without restriction is the mantra of the Democratic Party. And it is entirely reasonable to think that its own unshackled freedom was the main reason it lost the election. Wise people know when to apply the brakes. The United States' national debt is in the trillions of dollars. The economy would be a lot healthier if recent presidents practiced a little more fiscal restraint.

Being "unshackled" denotes a most dangerous condition. Something that is unshackled, like a pit bull terrier or an enraged bull, should be shackled for neither has the wit or wisdom to know when to stop as they ravage everything in their way, like General William Tecumseh Sherman in his march through Georgia. He did stop, however, once he got to the sea.

The great Anglo-Irish statesman and philosopher, Edmund Burke, shared his wisdom with posterity when he said, "But what is liberty without wisdom, and without virtue? It is the greatest of all possible evils; for it is folly, vice, and madness, without tuition or restraint."

Burke was not wimpy in his denunciation of unfettered freedom. He was also keenly aware that libertarian excesses spoil that which liberty should protect. Liberty should protect life, marriage, health, and the proper expression of human sexuality. Its profligacy, however, endangers them. In a relay race, one runner hands the baton to another. It is, in a sense, a sacrifice, but one that needed to attain victory.

Wisdom teaches us the order of values. It is akin to what we need when making a long journey. We need a car, then a train, then a taxi, and finally the airplane. When liberty has done its work, we call upon other values: gratitude, determination, care, and hospitality. If we expect too much from liberty, it will betray us. When we stop, it is only because we have the opportunity to do something else. We should not want liberty to snuff out succeeding values while making a mockery of itself. Wisdom teaches us when to stop and how to start anew.

Chapter 20

What is Existentialism?

What is existentialism is a frequent question people ask of philosophers. The word "existentialism" is intriguing and conveys a sense of mystery and the promise of an entirely new brand of thinking. The questioner may expect a simple and straightforward answer. Unfortunately, one is not available.

The truth of the matter is that the term "existentialism" applies to a wide consortium of thinkers who may be poles apart from each other. Nonetheless, by knowing something about existentialism, one deepens his understanding of the modern world.

In order to begin a preliminary understanding of existentialism, we must deal with two concepts that are at the heart of virtually every philosopher's thinking. They are "essence" and "existence". Essence refers to what something is—a tree, a fish, a human being, etc. Everything we know, we know in terms of its essence. It answers the simple question, "What is it?" Existence refers to the fact that things exist, which is to say that they stand outside of nothingness and are real.

Historians of philosophy agree that two philosophers in particular, Soren Kierkegaard (1813-1855) in Denmark and Fricdrich Nietzsche (1844-1900) in Germany, were the first modern existentialists. No two philosophers, however, could be more disparate, yet they both wear the mantle of existentialism.

Plato placed essences at the heart of his philosophy and created an interlocking system of ideas. He inaugurated a trend that culminated in the philosophy of George Friedrich Hegel who created an all-embracing system of ideas. Kierkegaard reacted strongly against this systematic kind of thinking. "I refuse to be a paragraph in a system," he declared, and emphasized the human being as a flesh and blood individual who exists and struggles to find meaning in a world of suffering. But, to exist authentically for the Danish thinker, means to live with love. "Existing," he proclaimed, "if this is to be understood as just any sort of existing, cannot be done without passion." Kierkegaard was intensely religious and installed hope as an essential virtue.

Nietzsche's philosophy is the perfect opposite of that of Kierkegaard. He introduced to the world "the death of God." He detested Christianity for its alleged moral weakness. Thrown back onto his own individual resources, he sought power through the independent exercise of his will. He looked to the emergence of a "super-man" (*Ubermensch*) who would rise to power through his own efforts. There is much in Nietzsche's thinking that was adopted by the Third Reich. Individual existence was at the core of his thinking. His specific type of existentialism logically leads to nihilism in which nothingness has dominion.

Two other important existentialist philosophers were also poles apart in their thinking: Jean-Paul Sartre (1905-1980) and Gabriel Marcel (1889-1973). Sartre's atheism leads directly to his rejection of all essences. He argues that since there is no God, there is no one to confer essences. Therefore, he concludes that there is no such thing as a human being. Essence, therefore, is something we create, not something we are given. Sartre, then, comes to his highly controversial conclusion that "existence precedes essence." Because there is no God and no nature (or essence) we are absolutely free to create our own essence in time. The fact that all our attention is riveted to the self is made clear in his famous dictum, "Hell is other people."

On the other hand, Gabriel Marcel, a Catholic convert, and critic of Sartrean philosophy reasoned that man is an existing essence—a human being that exists—and the meaning of his life is in service to others. He speaks of people being "present" to each other, and how they can be "available" to each other," two words that have entered our modern way of speaking. He makes an important distinction between "being" and "having". For Marcel, "being" captures our existing essence and has primacy over "having". No amount of things that we can have (or possess) can compare with the fundamental dignity of our being as human beings created by God. He argues contra Sartre that the existence of God does not prevent us from being free. We are able to choose God freely.

For the Great Russian novelist, Fedor Dostoevsky, if there be no God, then all things are permitted. For Sartre, the denial of God is the beginning of man's self-development. Stated here is one of the central questions of the modern world. Was Adam better off in attempting to be God?

Jacques Maritain is the most important Catholic philosopher of the 20th century. He reasons that St. Thomas Aquinas is the supreme existentialist since, according to the Angelic Doctor, "existence is the perfection of perfections." All creatures are a unity of essence and existence. Whereas essence is readily knowable, existence is not.

Even though we are sure that we exist, we have no concept of it. It is, for Maritain, a "super-intelligible". Existence itself does not exist. It is essences that exist. How, then, does existence come about. For Maritain, speaking for Aquinas and the medieval scholastics, God's essence is to exist. In this case, His existence is eternal. God is the one being whose essence is to exist. He is also the being who confers existence on all His creatures.

Maritain regards the incomprehensible, absolute unity of essence and existence in God as the summit of both philosophy and theology, a position that is in essential agreement with the words God used in identifying himself to Moses: "*I Am Who Am.*"

V.

Politics

Chapter 21

The Duality of Potentiality

In March of 1929, a most extraordinary event took place in Berlin, the likes of which may never be equaled. A twelve-year-old prodigy by the name of Jehudi Menuhin performed, in succession, the violin concertos of Bach, Beethoven, and Brahms. For an encore, he played the last two movements of the Mendelssohn concerto.

When this spectacular performance concluded, none other than Albert Einstein, an amateur fiddler in his own right, embraced the young prodigy and said, "Now I know there is a God". "My dear Yehudi," he went on to say, "Tonight I see that the day of miracles is not over. Our dear old Jehovah is still on the job".

The "most famous kid on the planet," to quote his biographer, Humphrey Burton, was a prodigy on the scale of Mozart. Menuhin performed in a concert with the San Francisco Symphony Orchestra when he was seven. Four years later, he debuted in New York's famous Carnegie Hall. He is regarded as one of the finest violinists of the 20th century.

The word "miracle" is often used loosely. Einstein, no doubt, used it advisedly. That night in Berlin six geniuses collaborated, like celestial objects pointing to the North Star, to produce an event that bears the signature of the Creator. Bach, Beethoven, Brahms, Mendelssohn, Menuhin, and Einstein blending together in one evening was a convocation that contained supernatural implications.

There is much talk these days about fulfilling one's potential. Unfortunately, this potential is often discussed at the expense of another potential, that of the child in the womb. No one knows what potential lies hidden in that sleeping child. President Biden has states that women have a right to abortion so that they can fulfill their potential. He does not understand the duality of potentiality.

The sextet of geniuses who convened that night in Berlin in March of 1929, were allowed to fulfill their respective potentialities thanks to their mothers' generous love. No one can underestimate the importance of giving birth to a child. In Christianity, Mary is the Mother of God. She consented to bring God into the world. What greater potential could ever be bestowed upon a woman?

While St. Thomas Aquinas was yet unborn, a holy hermit, known as Buono, went to the Castle of Rocca Secca and presented a prophecy to his expectant mother: "Lady be glad, for you are about to have a son whom you will call Thomas. You and your husband will think of making him a monk in the Abbey of Mount Cassino, where lies the founder, St Benedict, in the hope that your son will attain to its honours and wealth. But God has disposed otherwise, because he will become a Friar of the Order of Preachers. And so great will be his learning and sanctity, that there will not be found in the whole world, another person like him!" Hearing these words, Countess Theodora was amazed and, falling on her knees, exclaimed, "I am most unworthy of bearing such a son, but God's will be done according to His good pleasure!"

What God has in store for us exceeds our powers of imagination. I like to think that on that special night in Berlin nearly one hundred years ago, the mothers of Bach, Beethoven, Brahms, and Mendelssohn were spiritually present, supremely pleased that they had been granted the God-given potential to bring this quartet of musical geniuses into existence which, in turn, brought a treasure of musical beauty for the world to cherish. Their accomplishments perfectly coincided with the accomplishment of their sons.

Chapter 22

How Politics Can Smother Philosophy

In today's world, philosophy and politics, which should be in harmony with each other, are widely separated. The philosopher, acting in accord with his proper vocation, seeks the truth of things. The politician seeks to be elected. The philosopher's orientation is outward, while the politician's orientation is inward. The philosopher distinguishes between true and false; the politician distinguished between "right" and "left". The philosopher writes for journals that are seldom read by the man on the street. The politicians direct their rhetoric directly to the man on the street. The philosopher writes in solitude; the politician speaks from a stage.

Philosophy and politics, which should be married to each other, have been torn asunder to the point that philosophy has now become the enemy of politics. The problem is exacerbated in that politics, by dividing people into "right" and "left," is divided against itself. Furthermore, the notions of "right" and "left" are highly ambiguous.

Fr. Alphonse de Valk, C. S. B., while prefect at St. Joseph's College in Edmonton, Alberta, worked conscientiously for better salaries for his employees. The fact that he was widely known as a pro-life advocate caused some confusion among students. How can a right-wing person be concerned about people's salaries, they wondered? Similarly, Rev. John Richard Neuhaus, an ally of Martin Luther King who fought for civil rights, was also staunchly pro-life. The right/left categories could not capture him. One could say about him, what Jacques Maritain said about himself, "I am neither left nor right".

The confusion about how to categorize activists such as de Valk, Neuhaus, and others, is resolved simply by employing the philosophical word "justice". Justice for the unborn is perfectly harmonious with justice for the poor, the oppressed, and the underprivileged. The categories, "right" and "left," are too narrow to accommodate those who practice justice for all. Philosophy is broader than political categories, but politics, in smothering philosophy, has created a way in which people can be falsely represented. The same can be said about the categories, "conservative" and "liberal". If a person is "just," he should be regarded as being just and not squeezed into a category that misrepresents him.

Another verity that politics has smothered is "truth." People who avoid the word are prodigal in using the word "lie," as in calling one another, "liars." Using the word is an affirmation of truth, for a lie is a deviation from the truth. How can a person tell a lie is there is no truth which the lie misrepresents?

A student once said to me, "I shy away from absolutes." I should have said to him, "And I shy away from relatives." The pun is intended, but the larger point is that there can be no relatives if there are no absolutes, since what is relative is, by definition, related to an absolute. Then, if there are no relatives, there is nothing. My student, on the pretense of being philosophical, was telling me that there is no such thing as philosophy since there is no reality to serve as its object. In this case, my student was using his ego to smother philosophy. The ego can, indeed, be ruinous. Walter Lippman once said

Chapter 22: How Politics Can Smother Philosophy

that "Self-importance has ruined more good journalists than bad liquor."

Kamala Harris, much to the annoyance of her critics has used the expression "unburdened by what has been" so often that it sounds like a broken record. "I can imagine what can be when we are unburdened by what has been." Does she realize that by saying this, she impugns her own ancestry, including her parents? She speaks, however, with an air of triumph as if her tiresome mantra is convincing. It is characteristic of the "left" to denigrate the past and glorify the future. Harris carries this to an extreme. Have we nothing to learn from the past? If we "unburden" ourselves from what has been, is there a basis on which we can build a better future." Attend to the words of Sir Roger Scruton, regarded by popular intelligence as "conservative": "We do not merely study the past: we inherit it, and inheritance brings with it not only the rights of ownership, but the duties of trusteeship. Things fought for and died for should not be idly squandered. For they are the property of others, who are not yet born. . . Those who lose respect for the dead have ceased to be trustees of their inheritance. Inevitably, therefore, they lose the sense of obligation to future generations. The web of obligations shrinks to the present tense."

It is a self-destructive superstition that we can re-start society and this time do it right, that having scrapped the past, we can go forward, unburdened, and create through sheer will power, a happier and more humane society. This, of course, is political madness.

Philosophy, though suppressed, is, in the final analysis unsinkable. Truth, justice, and a commonsense view of reality cannot be completely expunged from the human soul. The past is not a burden, it is our inheritance, our birthright, that which gives us hope. It is our fuel for tomorrow. History sets the context for the present and the past, or as Shakespeare stated in The Tempest, "What's past is prologue." A Dutch historian once proclaimed that, "No other discipline has its portals so wide open to the general public as history." And these portals cannot be closed.

Chapter 23

How to Destroy America

Like everything else, so it seems, the LGBTQ+ consortium is divided into "liberal and "conservative". Once truth is removed from the discussion, opinions dominate and are inevitably separated into "right" and "left". Truth, however, has no "liberal/conservative" or "right/left" division. It provides a basis that is valid for everyone. Truth is indivisible. And, as Christ tells us, it is the Truth and nothing else that makes us free. America is no longer the "land of the free and the home of the brave." It has become the land of opinions and the home of the opinionated. As a result, the battle rages without any possible resolution in sight.

Writing for the September 9, 2024 issue of *Newsweek,* Tim Moran states that, "Harris and Walz are crusaders for a small but powerful cabal of the LGBT Left which wants to erase the concept of biological sex from society, expose young children to overtly sexualized and ideological content, and strip parents of their rights to make critical decisions about their children." Should we, then, support the Right Wing of the LGBTQ+ movement even though its only credit is that it is not Left Wing?

The curious thing about America is that equality is applied not to equals but to those things that cannot be equal. Hence, the human unborn are not accorded human rights, even though they are equally human with all other human beings, and things that are not equal, such as a traditional marriage and a same-sex marriage, are regarded as equal. This flip-flopping of equality opens the door to no end of mayhem. It generates a civil war in which peace is inconceivable.

We need not divide the LGBTQ+ brigade. It is criticisable on its generic terms. Sexual deviance cannot equated with what is sexually normal. The two are eternally separated by the natural law. What Harris and Walz are hoping to do is to erase the time-honored distinction between what is normal and what is deviant and make the two equal. This erasure, unfortunately, would unleash every malevolence that has been the good sense for people throughout history to keep in check by law or by custom. It would be enough to destroy America. The plain truth is that not every sexual act is normal. AIDS and the pandemic of sexually transmitted diseases is sufficient proof of this.

The Democratic Party is now routinely labelled a "culture of death." Kamela Harris's unbridled enthusiasm for abortion, at least in her mind, places abortion on an equal plane with live birth. But life and death are not, nor can they ever be, made equal. As St. Paul has iterated, light and darkness have nothing in common (2 Corinthians, 6: 14). Being and nothingness cannot be brought into harmony. Abortion and birth are both equally choice, but they are not equal in action or in outcome.

America is suffering from the delusion that all things can be compromised. Although He was tempted, Christ refused to make any compromises with the Devil. After He had fasted for 40 days and 40 nights, the Devil tempted Him to make compromises with the secular world. At last, Christ said to him, "Away from me, Satan! For it is written: Worship the Lord your God. And serve him only" (Matthew 4:9). There can be no compromise between God and the Devil.

Chapter 23: How to Destroy America

There is nothing neither in their thoughts nor actions that could possibly be equalized.

Politics has become the vain attempt to find the cow that has already left the barn. In failing to locate the cow, politicians use the straw as an ersatz cow. They then wonder why the straw cannot give milk.

Erasing the distinction between what is normal and what is deviant does not widen the frontier of liberty; it surrenders liberty to chaos. Alexander Solzhenitsyn was correct when he told his readers, in *The Error of the West*, that, "Time has eroded your notion of liberty. You have kept the word but devised a different notion. You have forgotten the meaning of liberty." Liberals speak of liberty but what they are promoting is slavery. "Of all the loose terms in the world," wrote Edmund Burke, "liberty is the most indefinite." "Liberty," he added, "must be secured by the equality of restraint." But restraint is precisely what today's liberal does not want. They believe that liberty is broadened every time a restraint is loosened.

Political leaders now employ words that have lost their meaning. Unfortunately, people fail to realize how these golden words—liberty, equality, justice, marriage--no longer mean what they are supposed to men. A new world is smuggled in through the conjunction of demagoguery and ignorance.

The Harris/Walz team speaks as though nature does not exist. But nature is inextinguishable and provides grounds for universal agreement and a restraint that prevents thought from escaping reality. Perhaps Cicero said it best: *Numquam naturam mos vinceret; est enim ea semper invicta*" (Custom will never conquer nature; indeed, nature will always conquer custom).

Biology, an aspect of nature, persists, and cannot be displaced by politics. There are two sexes, male and female, that are related to each other in a complementary fashion. Marriage is between a man and a woman. Abortion kills a human being. Children are not prepared to make life-long decisions. The traditional family is natural. By removing nature, reality is denied and there is nothing left to hold a nation together. No country can withstand such a maneuver.

Chapter 24

The Fragility of Democracy

After a failed assassination attempt on a presidential candidate, the terrifying question is put into focus as to whether American democracy will be sustained by the ballot or sabotaged by the bullet? In the aftermath of the Civil War, Abraham Lincoln had every good reason to declare that "Ballots are the rightful, and peaceful, successors of bullets".

Yes, indeed, but not everyone thinks this way. When G. K. Chesterton was a young journalist on the *Daily News*, he stated that, "Clapham, like every other city, is built on a volcano". His immediate superior glowered at him in a resentful manner. But G. K. had a point. There is a fault line that runs through every town and country. Its name may be Mt. Vesuvius or another volatile name.

"The ignorance of one voter in a democracy," said President John F. Kennedy, "impairs the security of all". In retrospect, his words appear to be ominously prescient. After his assassination, there were two assassination attempts on his successor, Gerald Ford.

In American history, four presidents were assassinated, Abraham Lincoln, James Garfield, William McKinley, and John F. Kennedy. In addition, there were attempts or plots to assassinate Andrew Jackson, Theodore Roosevelt, FDR, Harry Truman, William Howard Taft, Herbert Hoover, Richard Nixon, Jimmy Carter, Ronald Reagan, George H. W. Bush, Bill Clinton, George W. Bush, Barack Obama, and Donald Trump. In the words of Shakespeare, "Uneasy lies the head that wears the crown" (*King Henry IV*).

In his Gettysburg Address, Lincoln famously defined democracy as "that government of the people, by the people, and for the people". If we give more specific meaning to the three prepositions, then, democracy *belongs* to the people, is *produced* by the people, and is for the *benefit* of the people. Democracy is to be so highly prized, according to Lincoln, that it "should not perish from the earth".

How long democracy will last in America is contingent upon a number of factors, the most important of which is education. In the words of Franklin Delano Roosevelt, "Democracy cannot succeed unless those who express their choice are prepared to choose wisely. The real safeguard of democracy, therefore, is education".

Democracy originated in ancient Greece. Socrates, the Gadfly of Athens, who asked too many disturbing questions, was found guilty, by a democratic process, of impiety against the pantheon and corrupting the youth. The vote was 280 to 220 against him. He was then sentenced to death. It is not surprising, therefore, that Socrates regarded democracy as nearly the worst form of rule, although superior to tyranny. In the modern world, Winston Churchill famously stated that "democracy is the worst form of government, except all those other forms that have been tried from time to time". Aristotle fled Athens because he did not want his countrymen to "sin twice against philosophy".

If democracy, in the best sense, rests upon education, it currently rests on shaky grounds. Relativism has, for the most part, replaced philosophy, and the prevailing ethos consists off a strange blend of woke, cancel culture, diversity, inclusivity, and political correctness. For some educators, Shakespeare should be eliminated from the curriculum so that the reading list can be more "inclusive". Karl Marx stated that people become more easily manipulated when they are cut off from their tradition. G. K. Chesterton extended democracy to those who have preceded us: "Tradition is only democracy extended through time. It is trusting to a consensus of common human voices rather than to some isolated or arbitrary record . . . Tradition means giving votes to the most obscure of all classes, our ancestors. It is the democracy of the dead. Tradition refuses to submit to the small and arrogant oligarchy of those who merely happen to be walking about".

John Patrick Diggins is "Distinguished Professor of History at the Graduate Center of the City University of New York. He is the author of numerous books including, *The Rise and fall of the American Left*. In his book, *On Hallowed Grounds*, he draws a rather bleak picture of the contemporary American mindset: "Never before in American history has there been such confusion about the meaning of America and the identity of the American people. Never before have Americans been so deprived of the backward glance of historical understanding unsullied by the idiocy of political correctness".

Education must include a knowledge of history, an appreciation of the arts, an acquaintance with philosophy, and a grasp of logic. It must also gain some understanding and respect for religion. Perhaps, most of all, a sound ethic should be taught which stresses the nature of justice and truth. Students are currently being indoctrinated in the direction of totalitarianism. Abortion is a good example of this tendency. Significant people in power cannot tolerate the existence of a pro-life contingent. Innocent advocates for life are punished and jailed for their beliefs. Some authorities have branded them as "terrorists". A famous actress has suggested that all pro-lifers should be put to death. Anyone who is involved in the defense of pre-natal life realizes all too well that he is not operating in a democratic milieu. The obvious trend is toward a totalitarian state where legitimate, but politically incorrect opinions, are not allowed.

Democracy is fragile. Its survival needs those impassioned words in the national anthem to be put into practice: "And crown thy good with brotherhood from sea to shining sea".

> "Democracy is a device that ensures we shall be governed no better than we deserve." George Bernard Shaw

Chapter 25

The Radical Change in the Conscience of America

In 1980 Ronald Reagan defeated Jimmy Carter in a landslide victory amassing 489 Electoral College votes to become America's 40th president. Four years later, he was re-elected, defeating Walter Mondale, carrying 525 Electoral College votes. Reagan captured every state except Minnesota, where Mondale was governor.

In the decade of the eighties Reagan was truly America's president. It might be said that he personified the conscience of the country he was chosen to lead. Three years into his first term, he authored *Abortion and the Conscience of the Nation* in which he stated his firm commitment to the sanctity of life that included those human beings residing in their mothers' wombs. In 2024 Kamala Harris ran for president stating forcefully and univocally that a national abortion law was first and foremost on her agenda. She accorded it top priority over economic and foreign policy concerns. Her running mate, Tim Walz, shared her view on abortion and argued for a national abortion right, stripping all states of their right to decide the abortion issue in the voting booth. When he was president, Obama was a forceful proponent of abortion while President Biden promoted abortion as if it was the most important thing in the world. He called the perfectly legitimate overturning of *Roe v. Wade,* 'outrageous'.

In the 40 some years between Reagan and Harris, has the conscience of America undergone such a proportionate change in its attitude toward the sanctity of life? It may be of some interest to revisit Reagan's essay and assess how far apart one president and a presidential candidate are over a span of 40 years on the issue of the sanctity of life. Cultural is dynamic, constantly shifting in its attitudes and convictions. The change concerning the attitude toward the sanctity of life can serve as a barometer indicating where the nation is headed.

Time magazine noted that "An essay by a recent sitting President is rare." But is even more rare for the President to make a strong pronouncement on a moral issue. Reagan was concerned that his essay might be judged as pontificating on a single issue. With this possible criticism in mind, he explained that "Abortion concerns not only the unborn child, it concerns every one of us." And indeed it does, being intimately involved with marriage, the family, the medical and law professions, education, society in general, as well as posterity. Abortion bears upon the future.

It was appropriate that the President should release his statement on the tenth anniversary of *Roe v. Wade*. It was an auspicious time for Americans "to pause and reflect." The infamous 1973 decision was not voted for by the American people nor was it enacted by their legislators. At that time not a single state permitted unrestricted abortion. The *Roe v. Wade* decision did not reflect the conscience of the nation. "Make no mistake," Reagan added, "abortion-on-demand is not a right granted by the constitution." The 1973 ruling was, in the biting phrase of Justice White, "an act of raw judicial power."

In the field of medicine, the unborn child is regarded as a patient. This is a fact that should not be ignored. In one remarkable case, an unborn child underwent brain surgery six times during the months prior to his birth. "Who is the *patient*?" Reagan asks, "if not that tiny unborn human being who can feel pain when he or she is approached by doctors who come to kill rather than to cure?"

The abortion mentality presents a slippery slope that slides into infanticide. In the case of Baby Doe, which was brought to national attention, a child was allowed to die even though a routine surgical procedure would have saved his life because he had Down Syndrome. A doctor, testifying during court procedures, stated that Baby Doe would have a "non-existent" possibility for "a minimally adequate quality of life." "In other words," Reagan writes, "retardation was the equivalent of a crime deserving the death penalty." The judge permitted Baby Doe to starve to death and the Indiana Supreme Court approved the decision.

President Reagan went into action. He directed the departments of Justice and Health and Human services to protect handicapped newborns. After the Baby Doe incident, all hospitals receiving federal funds would be required to post notices clearly stating that failure to feed handicapped babies is prohibited by federal law.

Reagan cited a former president who had an unflagging respect for the Declaration of Independence that spoke of all men being created equal and "endowed by their Creator with certain unalienable rights" including life, and liberty. Abraham Lincoln praised the framers of that noble document stating that "In their enlightened belief, nothing stamped with the divine image and likeness was sent into the world to be trodden on." Lincoln wisely understood that if rights were denied of one group (Blacks), they could very well be denied of another group (the unborn). Therefore, as the Declaration states, the God-endowed right to life should extend to everyone, healthy or handicapped, born or unborn.

President Reagan concludes his essay with an impassioned commitment to honoring the right to life of all human beings: "My administration is dedicated to the preservation of America as a free land, and there is no cause more important than affirming the transcendent right to life without which no other rights have any meaning."

In what state do we find the conscience of America at this moment in history? It is a state of unrest oscillating between a Reagan/Lincoln model and one concocted by Biden and Harris. May God bless and protect the former model as American moves into an uncertain future.

VI.

Religion

Chapter 26

The Primacy of Faith

It is not unusual to find in college textbooks a convenient division of Western history into three periods. The first is the period that belongs to the Greeks and their remarkable accomplishments in philosophy, literature, astronomy, and morality. It was a period which saw the triumph of knowledge and harmony. The second period, the Middle Ages, is described as the Dark Ages. It was a time in which Christianity flourished, but also a time when blind faith supposedly obscured the normal use of natural reason. Since God has spoken, there is no longer any need for man to think. Toward the end of the 15th century a period of rational inquiry began, which was the dawn of science. The prodigious development of science has continued unabated to the present.

It becomes surprising, even shocking, to some that eminent scientists have stressed the importance of faith. Norbert Wiener, for example, the founding thinker of cybernetics theory, explains to his fellow scientists how faith is primary. In his book, *The Human Use of Human Beings* (1950) he speaks of faith in the Augustinian tradition and points out that scientists need to have faith that the world they study is intelligible. The fact that the world is, indeed, intelligible, cannot be proven. It must be accepted on faith.

Alfred North Whitehead, co-author of *Mathematica Principia*, and a student of history, expresses the indebtedness the modern world has to the Middle Ages. In his book, *Science and the Modern*

World, he points out that "the faith in the possibility of science, generated antecedently to the development of modern scientific theory, is an unconscious derivation from medieval theology." Faith and knowledge are not mutually antagonistic. The so-called Dark Ages was an important contributor to today's period of science.

Einstein's famous comment that "God does not play dice with the world" indicates that his faith in the orderliness of the universe was something that science could not prove but was nonetheless credible. His faith is also borne out when he states that the most incomprehensible feature of the universe is that it is comprehensible.

The primacy of faith, enunciated by various scientists is perfectly consistent with the famous formula of St. Anselm: *credo ut intelligam* (I believe so that I may understand). We begin with the faith that our intellectual pursuits are not in vain, but worthwhile. Faith is exonerated when so many of the things that we know fit together. The pieces of the puzzle depict a unified whole. Our faith becomes fully justified.

Philosophy is the love of wisdom. This simple phrase presupposes that we have the capacity to love and that wisdom is attainable. We cannot get started without faith. We believe that we can love and also believe that wisdom is attainable. Our life, if lived properly, is a series of justifications of our faith. We need faith to get out of bed in the morning, to marry, to have children, to attend a particular school, or to become a scientist.

Pope John Paul's encyclical, *Fides et Ratio* (Faith and Reason) begins with these towering words: "Faith and reason are like two wings on which the human spirit rises to the contemplation of truth; and God has placed in the human heart a desire to know the truth—

in a word, to know himself—so that, by knowing and loving God, men and women may also come to the fullness of truth about themselves".

Faith is a virtue that, despite being under-rated in the modern world, is essential as a prelude to virtually everything we do. And the most insightful of scientists must tip his cap to faith because, without it, he could not get started.

Chapter 27

Do We Need the Ten Commandments?

The Jews had been Pharaoh's slaves and subject to his barbarous treatment for a period of 400 years. They could not possibly have been moral relativists. They understood with unmistakable clarity that their captivity was morally wrong, and they yearned to be free. The Pharaoh's ways were not God's ways and God chose Moses to deliver them from bondage.

Ironically, the Jews used their new found freedom to enslave themselves in a different way. "They have been quick to turn away from what I commanded them," said God, "and have made themselves an idol cast in the shape of a calf. They have bowed down to it and sacrificed to it and have said, 'These are your gods, Israel, who brought you up out of Egypt'." While Moses was away for some time, his people were shamelessly indulging in "revelry." They had become slaves to their own sins.

It was evident that they needed a better set of rules. The Jews were not created to be self-indulgent. Hence, God presented them with the Ten Commandments as a way of teaching them how to live righteously. An important lesson to be drawn from *Exodus* is that the blessing of the Commandments is dramatically contrasted with the degeneracy of dancing around an idol. Furthermore, the commandments were not options or mere opinions, they were issued by the authority of God and must be obeyed. There was no thought of "imposing" values. The Commandments were issued for the benefit of the Jews. When the Commandments were rejected, debauchery followed.

The story line in *Exodus* makes it clear that human beings need guidance from above. Left to their own resources, they fall astray. Morality is not an arbitrary set of rules. It is a requirement without which people cannot be truly human, properly civilized, or fully alive. The fact that Moses needed to ascend the mountain twice indicates the hard-heartedness of man and how reluctant he is to live a moral existence.

Throughout history, the need for the Ten Commandments has been refuted in different ways. Foremost among its refutations is the notion that they repudiate our freedom. One might say that nobody, not even God can tell me what to do or how to live. Nonetheless the Commandments do not oppose freedom itself, but the wrong use of freedom, as illustrated by the Jews wildly dancing around the Golden Calf.

Contemporary deconstructionists claim that the Ten Commandments are based on the existence of God. But if God does not exist, then the commandments are deconstructed and are bereft of any authority. Then, people are free to do as they please. Atheistic existentialists, such as Jean Paul Sartre, absolutize freedom and are not open to anyone else's advice.

Human beings are reluctant to heed the Commandments as suggested by the following witticism: A scheming lawyer says, "I have some good news and some bad news. Which do you want to hear first"? "The good news," the audience replies. "I have managed to reduce the 15 Commandments to ten." "Hooray," cries the crowd." "And the bad news, importunes the crowd"? "Adultery is still in."

Chapter 27: Do We Need the Ten Commandments?

Even St. Augustine implored God to make him chaste, but "not yet." Hollywood celebrity, Carl Reiner, reduced the Ten Commandments to one: "Don't hurt anyone." Unfortunately, this lone negative edict fails to tell us what we should do.

Do we really need revelation? St. Thomas Aquinas, in his monumental *Summa Theologica*, states that "It was necessary for man's salvation that there should be a knowledge revealed by God, besides philosophical science built up by human reason. . . . Even as regards those truths about God which human reason could have discovered, it was necessary that man should be taught by a divine revelation; because the truths about God such as reason could discover, would only be known by a few, and that after a long time, and with the admixture of many errors" (I, 1).

Another problem concerning the Ten Commandments has to do with whether they are good in themselves or whether they are arbitrary edicts in the sense that God could change them according to His whims. A fourteenth century philosopher by the name of William of Ockham argued that there could have been a contradictory set of Commandments that would be equally binding since the point of any of God's Commandments to obey them. According to this view, the Commandments are good because they were made by God. In this way, in requiring obedience, God was illustrating His power. The view of Aquinas and others is that God created the Commandments because they were good in themselves. Hence, God was motivated by love since He wanted what is best for his creatures.

A burning question, for a long time, is whether the Ten Commandments have any place in secular schools. As of June 19, 2024, and with the authority of Governor Jeff Landry, Louisiana became the first state to require that the Ten Commandments be displayed in every public school classroom. The Commandments would be in a "large, easily readable font" on posters 11 inches by 14 inches. Not surprisingly, the move has come under fire, being denigrated as "conservative." However, it should be reiterated that the Ten Commandments is not at all political. It is a moral statement that pertains to everyone.

What harm can there be in reminding students, in a way that is unspoken, that respecting God and parents, not stealing or killing, and avoiding greed and lust is worthy of their attention? America is presently suffering from loose morals. It is time for the Ten Commandments to make a curtain call.

Chapter 28

Has Genesis Been Deconstructed?

Deconstructionism is more of a trend than a philosophy. It is based on the notion that language is incapable of defining objects. Therefore, what we have naively constructed is not entirely reliable and must be deconstructed. Once deconstruction has its way, nothing is left standing. It is like knocking over the construction your little brother has made. Deconstructionism itself may be deconstructed because it harbors an elementary contradiction. Its advocates expect to be understood while they contend that all messages are unintelligible.

Religious belief is especially vulnerable to being deconstructed since its foundation is said to be uncertain. Deconstructionist Jonathan Culler, for example, claims that "religious discourse" and "theistic beliefs" do not "deserve respect, any more than we would assume that sexist or racist beliefs deserve respect." In particular, the deconstruction of the story of creation as presented in the *Book of Genesis*, is of special concern in today's confused world.

The meaning of five specific assertions at the heart of the *Book of Genesis* are being emptied today of their original intent: 1) that God saw that his creation was good; 2) that God saw that it is not good for man to be alone; 3) that God created human beings male and female; 4) that mother and father are properly identified as such; 5) that marriage is a union between a husband and a wife.

In Psalm 113:5 we read, "Who is like the Lord our God who is enthroned on high?" Implicit in this verse is the supremacy of God.

There is no other authority that can be compared with the Lord, our God. It would be blasphemous for anyone to belief that he could rival God. In stating that creation is "good," God indicates that it does not stand to be improved. But once the supremacy of God is deconstructed, human beings attempt to supply what the Divinity presumably neglected. This hubris is manifested in points 2 to 5.

God saw, in contrast with nature, that it was *not* good for man to be alone. Adam suffered in his solitude, longing for a mate. As a corollary, it is also not good for man to remain in his subjectivity as a thinker. Attempting to conceive a coherent philosophy solely through one's own efforts is doomed to failure. James Sale, author of more than 50 books, makes the comment that "We have engineered a world in which complete subjectivity has replaced traditional values and scientific authority. And for the 'believers,' this is their religion." This "complete subjectivity" accords with Adam's rejection of God.

From time immemorial the various nations of the world accepted the presumed fact that human beings are either male or female. It is now politically correct to believe that such a view is entirely subjective. One's gender is no longer thought of as something that nature has decreed, but as something that one chooses. The Ontario Human Rights commission has defined gender identity as "each person's internal and individual experience of gender. It is the sense of being as a woman, a man, both, neither, or anywhere along the gender spectrum." Individuals living in New York City can choose from a minimum of 31 different gender identities. It has been estimated that there may be as many as 63 different genders. Under the rules of New York City's commission on Human Rights, businesses risk incurring fines up to $250,000 for failing to respect and accommodate a person's chosen gender identity. Supreme Court Justice Nominee, Ketanji Brown Jackson, admitted that she could not define the word "woman" when asked to do so during the Senate hearing. President Biden, however, had nominated her precisely because she was a woman.

The terms "mother" and "father" have undergone significant changes. "Mother" has been replaced by "birthing person" or "Progenitor A." In the world of reproductive technology, the courts have been called upon to determine who the legal mother is. Is it the one who supplies the egg, the one who gestates the child, the one who gives birth, or the one who raises the child? "Father" has been reduced to "donor" or "Progenitor B."

In the interest of abolishing the distinctiveness of maternal breastfeeding, the neologism "chest-feeding" has been created. In this way, men will not be discriminated because, with new technologies, they, too, can "chest-feed". The invitation of trans-men, trans-women, and those that are non-binary has prompted some members of La Leche League to resign. They maintained that breastfeeding should be restricted to mothers, an attitude that is making its way toward oblivion.

On June 26, 2015, the United States Supreme Court ruled, in a 5-4 decision, that the Fourteenth Amendment requires all states to grant same-sex marriages. The Court rendered this decision despite the fact that defining the nature of marriage was beyond its purview. By 2022 there were roughly 740,500 same-sex married couples in the United States. It is difficult to understand the meaning of marriage in today's society since its participants can assume any of several types of gender identities. Marriage between a man and a woman is now commonly referred to as a "traditional" marriage. This dubious term suggests that it is a thing of the past and not in step with our progress age. The words 'husband' and 'wife' now seem atavistic.

The present deconstruction of *Genesis* is well underway. God's Word is no longer compelling. But it has been replaced with an anything goes mentality which cannot possibly serve society well.

Genesis is about the 'beginning.' One has reason to fear that its rejection in the modern world signals the 'end'. Deconstruction leads to nihilism.

Chapter 29

Who Is Left to Defend Genesis?

The Kinks is an English rock band sufficiently proficient to have been inducted into the Rock and Roll Hall of Fame. One of the band's numbers, *Lola*, is actually a defence of *Genesis*: "Girls will be boys and boys will be girls. It's a mixed up, muddled up, shook up world." It may be a misfortune that the group disbanded in 1996. Who is left, then, in our confused world to defend *Genesis*?

After God created the world, He said that it was "good." Today's gurus are saying, "He could have done better." The creator's mistake was to make a distinction between men and women. He should have been motivated by a higher principle, namely, "equality." All the important people now know that inequality breeds discrimination. Therefore, we should eliminate divisive pairings such as boy/girl, men/women, husband/wife, and father/mother. Equality should be our new guiding star.

Elizabeth Badinter, the intellectual heir of feminist icon, Simone de Beauvoir, dismisses God, as well as *Genesis*, as irrelevant, and rejects the complementarity model of the sexes as archaic. She argues that whenever sexual asymmetry has been put into practice, men dominated women. Inequality between the sexes, in her estimation, always leads to domination and oppression. As an indication of culture's growing "emancipation" from the plane of the biological, she alludes to an emerging attitude claiming the "right to incest."

Badinter recognized that as long as men could not procreate, inequality between the sexes would persist. Therefore, she proposed a "sharing" form of pregnancy in which the embryo would be transferred from the female body to the male body and then back to the female who would give birth to the child. She also considers men giving birth through Caesarian section. For Badinter, all this shuffling back and forth the between male and female during pregnancy makes sense. "It is hard to grasp," she writes in *Man/Woman*, "the philosophical and moral principles behind the rejection of this hypothesis."

The shared pregnancy, unnatural in its conception, would pose significant dangers to the female, the male, and the child. Nonetheless, in Badinter's mind, these dangers would be offset by the achievement of a more equal relationship between men and women. Surely, the *Genesis* description of marriage as a two-in-one flesh unity between a man and a women, presumably belongs to the distant past.

The equality ideology has made its way into the nature of marriage. The same-sex marriage is promoted as being equal with the marriage between a man and a woman. Canada Post has issued a stamp that proclaims the equality between both forms of marriage. Justices of the peace have lost their jobs when refusing to bless a same-sex marriage. The United States Supreme Court has upheld this new concept of marriage, even though rendering decisions on the nature of marriage is far beyond the ambit of the Supreme Court. What was unthinkable only a few years ago has caught on and has grown exponentially. In 2022 there were roughly 740,500 same-sex married couples in the United States.

The La Leche League was founded to assist mothers in breast feeding their infants. The neologism "chestfeeding" has been

Chapter 29: Who Is Left to Defend Genesis?

adopted in some hospitals in the interest of establishing equality between men and women. "Chestfeeding" is a more inclusive term that embraces trans-men, transwomen, and those who are non-binary. The international board of La Leche League recently directed all British affiliates to begin accommodating men who believe they are women. This attitude has not set well with members of the La Leche League. Marian Thompson, 94, who founded the League, along with another high-level member, has resigned over the board's decision to allow men who believe they are women to participate in the organization's breastfeeding support groups. She contends that the decision is "a travesty of my original intent."

The LGBTQ+ consortium, in the interest of equality, argues that men are capable of breastfeeding babies as a result of taking synthetic hormones. It is not known, however, how this form of breastfeeding will affect the babies. According to Thompson, "This shift from following the norms of nature, which is the core of mothering through breastfeeding, to indulging the fantasies of adults, is destroying our organization."

Nature has the quality of solidity whereas equality is a mere abstraction. Forcing equality on things that are essentially unequal is like trying to force a square peg into a round whole. *Genesis* speaks respectfully about nature. When God completed His creation, as mentioned above, in the words of *Genesis* 1:31, "Then God looked over all he made and he saw that it was good!" It is not possible to improve on the works of God. Equality has its place. We are equally human beings and equal under the law. But the attempt to force things that are radically different into an artificially concocted equality mold is an act of treason against God and His creation. It is a way of taking something that is essentially good and turning it into something that is essentially unworkable. It is the theology of the devil who despises God's creation. As Aristotle has pointed out, "The worst form of inequality is to try to make unequal things equal."

Genesis is archaic only in the sense that it was written long ago. But it is not archaic in the sense that its message is eternal and relevant for all ages. God never goes out of date.

Chapter 30

A Brief Introduction to the Life of Edith Stein/ Saint Teresa Benedicta of the Cross

Edith Stein was born in Breslau, Germany, on October 12, 1891. She was the youngest of eleven children of a devout Jewish family. From an early age Edith displayed remarkable intelligence. She enjoyed the tutelage she received from her eldest brother who would carry her about in his arms, lecturing her on Goethe, Schiller, and other German poets and playwrights. When her older sister and her friends played 'Authors,' the four-year-old prodigy knew all the answers at once. She was precocious, but she was not without vanity.

It may be that her intellectual enthusiasms outpaced her interest in matters of faith. At age 14, she declared herself an atheist. Christianity first came into her purview when her Germanic studies led her to read the Lord's Prayer in Gothic. Her first intellectual encounter with faith came in the summer of 1913 when she heard a series of lectures given by Max Scheler, a Catholic convert from the Jewish faith. He made the case brilliantly that religion alone makes a human being human. "He poured forth Catholic ideas," she noted, "with the whole splendor of his mind and the whole power of his language." His words, however, "did not lead me to faith," she writes, "but they unlocked to me a province of 'phenomena' which I could no longer pass by blindly." Her rationalistic prejudice was dissolved "and suddenly there stood before me the world of faith."

In 1916, Edith Stein received her doctorate, *summa cum laude,* at Freiburg University, the subject of her dissertation being, *On the Problem of Empathy*. She had anticipated the one virtue that would be most needed during the period of the Third Reich. As a consequence of rejecting empathy--a feeling of connectedness with one's neighbor--the situation in Nazi Germany became dire. "Not human activity will help us," Dr. Stein stated, "but the passion of Christ. To partake in it is my desire."

She studied philosophy intensely, first phenomenology under Edmund Husserl and then the writings of St. Thomas Aquinas. Her passion for the truth never left her. "My yearning for the truth was one single prayer," she wrote. One day, while at the home of a friend, she went to his bookshelves and selected, quite at random, *The Life of St. Teresa of Avila*. It was the fortuitous confrontation of a saint of the past with a saint of the future. She was immediately captured and did not stop reading until she finished the book. "This is the truth," she said to herself. She was fortified by St. Teresa of Avila's promise: "Once one has tasted a single drop of the water of the Kingdom, he is repelled by the taste of anything earthly."

That same day, she purchased a catechism and a missal which she studied until she mastered them. Then she went to the parish church and attended Mass for the first time. "None of it was strange to me," she wrote, "Thanks to my previous reading, I understood every little ceremony." She waited for the celebrant to finish his thanksgiving and then followed him into the rectory. Without any preliminaries, she asked to be baptized. The priest was astonished by what must have seemed to him as an impulsive act and told her that she needed more preparation. Rather than capitulate to his reasonable advice, she asked to be examined on the spot. She did so well in this impromptu test that the priest arranged for her baptism on the first day of the New Year.

And so, on January 1, 1922, at the age of 30, Edith Stein was baptized, taking the name Teresa as her baptismal name. According to one observer, "She had the happiness of a child, and this was most beautiful!" A month later, on February 2, Candlemas Day, she was confirmed. Prior to her conversion, she assumed that one day she would be married. Her faith changed all that. She now had the interior conviction that she would become a Carmelite nun. And so, she did.

Her mother's reaction to Edith's conversion caught her off guard—she wept, something that Edith had never witnessed in her mother. Frau Stein had believed that Catholicism was a superstitious sect. In time, however, Frau Stein, who was a godly woman, could sense, though not comprehend, the holiness that was emanating from her daughter's being. Edith continued to attend the synagogue with her mother but prayed the psalms from the Roman breviary. "Never have I seen anyone pray as Edith did," her mother confessed.

She lived as a sister in the Carmelite convent in Cologne. Then, in the wake of *Kristallnacht* (the breaking of windows at a synagogue as part of a pogrom against Jewish people), in 1938, she fled to Holland and the Carmel at Echt. When the Nazi takeover in 1940 took place, Teresa Stein fully realized that Anti-Semitic persecution would intensify. She responded by asking God to accept her sacrifice as an offering for peace in the world. One day, and without warning, Nazi soldiers came to the convent door and gave Edith and her sister

10 minutes to pack before they were sent on a train bound for the concentration camp in Auschwitz.

On August 9, 1942, Edith and her sister, Rosa, also a convert, died in a gas chamber at Auschwitz. Pope John Paul II declared her Saint Teresa Benedicta of the Cross on October 11, 1998. The following year he proclaimed her "Co-Patroness of Europe. In 1942, Germany issued a hauntingly beautiful postage stamp honoring the saint, depicting her in her Carmelite habit.

Epilogue

None Are So Blind

The account in John 9:1-39 concerning the miraculous restoration of the sight of a man born blind attests to both the power of Jesus and the obtuseness of human beings.

As He was passing by, Jesus met a man who was blind from birth. His disciples asked whether this affliction was due to his sin or that of his parents. "Neither has this man sinned nor his parents", responded Jesus, "but the works of God were to be made manifest in him . . . As long as I am in the world I am the light of the world." After saying these words, Jesus spat on the ground and made clay with the spittle and spread the clay over the man's eyes. Then he bade him to wash in the pool of Siloe. The man did as he was directed and returned in full possession of his sight.

The miracle caused some confusion among the neighbors. Was this the same man "who used to sit and beg?" some asked. The man said, "I am he'. He was then taken to the Pharisees for further questioning. Some of them, however, rejected his testimony saying that "This man is not from God, for he does not keep the Sabbath". They were resorting to a technicality to dismiss an obviosity.

The miracle, in one sense, was too extraordinary to believe, but in addition to that, the Pharisees were unwilling to acknowledge that Jesus was the person He claimed to be. Their ruling status was being threatened. This was something that they could not surrender. The man whose sight was restored was then taken to his parents who were asked, "Is this your son, of whom, you say that he was born blind? How then does he now see?" The parents, however, were justifiably fearful and said, "He is of age; question him".

The man becomes subject to abuse and ultimately banished from the community. The interrogators had little interest in the facts of the case. Their strategy was to withhold official recognition of the healing by slandering Jesus in order to cover up the miracle. They made it all too clear, however, that they were unwilling to see what actually transpired. Accordingly, Jesus says, "For judgment have I come into this world, that they who do not see, may see and they who see may become blind". Restoring the sight of the man born blind was an example, though highly dramatic, of Jesus' desire to restore the spiritual sight of others.

The Pharisees, scribes, and high priests were imprisoned by their assumptions of superiority. Hence, they were incapable of seeing either their own vanity or the divinity of Jesus. The lower class, having no such assumptions, were better able to see what is essential. In this sense, Jesus can proclaim, "Blessed are the poor in spirit' (Matthew 5:3).

The intellectual blindness exhibited by the Pharisees and others in the account of the man born blind whose sight was miraculously restored, offers a prototype and a parable for a better understanding of the same blindness that afflicts various groups in the contemporary world. This group blindness inevitably makes dialogue unlikely.

Three groups in particular suffer from this specific form of blindness. In each case there is a withdrawing from reality because of fear. This fear prevents them from any honest discussion with their opponents.

The first is radical feminism. This ideology (and it is not a philosophy) is characterized by a rejection of the patriarchy which, if it were carried to its logical conclusion, would be self-destructive. It also includes a rejection or degradation of men along with the delusion that a woman is an independent, solo entity. Feminism has effectively barricaded itself against criticism. Despite its absence of reasonableness, however, it remains enormously influential.

The second group, the pro-abortion lobby, is also built on a false premise. It denies the human reality of the unborn, elevates choice to a self-justifying principle, and defames anyone who offers reasonable criticism. It remains willfully blind to the devastating effects that abortion has on women, men, and the family. It flies in the face of everything we know about embryology, fetology, sociology, and psychology. It is an island unto itself and brooks no criticism.

The third group consists of atheists who, as a matter of course, reject God. This rejection leaves them with very little truth with which to defend their position. Yet, the more formidable atheists of the modern world—Marx, Stalin, Lenin, Hitler, Feuerbach, Comte, Freud, Sartre, Nietzsche, Darwin—have been unreachable and unrelenting in their fidelity to their no-God philosophy. Their hostility to religion has been an unhappy side-effect of their atheistic outlook.

Trying to communicate with representatives of any of these three groups can be frustrating and futile. Jesus experienced this problem with the Pharisees and other leaders who closed themselves off from anything challenging. We learn from Jesus about the supreme importance of humility, not to take oneself too seriously, and to avoid a group mentality that is closed to anything different from itself. We also learn something about patience, understanding, and forgiveness. We learn that none are so blind as those who refuse to see. And we look into ourselves and discover how much darkness is there. We invite the light of Jesus as we try to remove the darkness in ourselves.

www.ingramcontent.com/pod-product-compliance
Lightning Source LLC
LaVergne TN
LVHW020932090426
835512LV00020B/3320